"And have no fellowship with the unfruitful works of darkness, but rather reprove them." *Ephesians 5:11*

Cults and Isms: TRUE or FALSE?

By Alan and Pat Franklin

"Then the LORD said unto me, the prophets prophesy lies in my name: I sent them not, neither have I commanded them, neither spoke unto them: they prophesy unto you a false vision and divination, and a thing of nought, and the deceit of their heart.

"Therefore thus saith the LORD concerning the prophets that prophesy in my name, and I sent them not, yet they say, sword and famine shall not be in this land; **by sword and famine shall those prophets be consumed.**

"And the people to whom they prophesy shall be cast out in the streets of Jerusalem because of the famine and the sword, and they shall have none to bury them, them, their wives, nor their sons, nor their daughters: for I will pour their wickedness upon them."

Jeremiah 14:14–16

There is a price to pay for following false prophets!

For information contact alan@thefreepressonline.co.uk.

ISBN 978-158712-197-5

Published by Banner LLC, St. Louis, Missouri
and World Wide Printing, TX
Printed by Printcorp in Minsk, Belarus. Ord. 2145 (09084)

TABLE OF CONTENTS

Introducing Our Exposé of Cults and Isms

by Alan Franklin

I normally speak and write about prophecy, starting with our first book, *EU: Final World Empire* and continuing with *Goodbye America, Goodbye Britain,* which gave a biblical framework for the tumultuous events unfolding before our eyes.

Pat and I also run a website, www.thefreepressonline.co.uk, which carries daily developments relevant to the Bible's prophecies, the Bible in the headlines.

These are exciting times, the end times, the times of the signs of the Lord's soon return!

Before this astounding event takes place, Jesus told us what to watch for. One of the signs — in evidence all round the world today — is the rapid rise in false cults and isms; non-biblical belief systems and evil, Satanically-inspired doctrines, like political correctness.

Matthew 24 sets the scene for the final acts to be played out on earth before He comes to put an end to false sects and philosophies. As the Lord sat on the Mount of Olives, overlooking Jerusalem, He answered the disciples' question (verse 3): "What shall be the sign of thy coming, and of the end of the world?"

The first response Jesus gave was a warning about deception: "Take heed that no man deceive you. For many shall come in my name, saying I am Christ; and shall deceive many." Jesus gave the warning about false Christs and prophets three times to show its importance *(Matthew 24: 5, 11 and 24).* In verse 24 He warns that these false teachers will show great signs and wonders and, if it were possible, will deceive even Christians — "the very elect." Today many people are easily deceived. So we wrote this book to shine some light into dark corners of the false sects and isms that often masquerade as Christian — and also into Islam.

Cults have been muddying the spiritual waters since the Judaizers in the first century AD, and false teaching within supposed Christianity really got under way with Constantine when he became a nominal Christian in 312 A.D., when a form of Christianity became the dominant religion of the Roman Empire, becoming the official religion in 380 A. D. Out of this came Romanism, the Roman Catholic Church, the biggest "ism" of all to this day, with over a billion followers. So we give a lot of space in this book to look at the false claims and doctrines of Catholicism.

We also examine the claims and beliefs of Islam, which now numbers more adherents than Catholicism. We test the claims of Mohammed and his followers against what the Bible says. Do we pray "to the same god," as we are told by politicians and churchmen? The answers are inside, in our second Table of Truth.

One of our Tables of Truth looks at the Mormons, the cult founded in the mid 19th century by Joseph Smith. These and Jehovah's Witnesses are those you are most likely to find on your doorstep, claiming to be Christians. Are they? We answer that question.

Also included are the Seventh Day Adventists, which may surprise some who assume they are just another type of Christian denomination. Having examined their background and teaching, we believe this is untrue: they have the characteristics of a cult. Interestingly, Charles Taze Russell, the JW founder, was influenced by the Millerites, forerunners of the Adventist cult. As well as making false prophecies about the end of the world, the return of the Lord etc, they both share the unscriptural doctrine of "soul sleep." There are often links or similarities between the founders of false faiths. Often, like the Mormon conman Joseph Smith and Ellen White, prophetess of Adventism, the occult plays a part in that they both "saw visions."(Mohammed had a similar experience in a cave.) They were clearly not hearing from God, as their visions were wayward and unbiblical. The reason for the links and similarities is that behind all false religion is the liar-in-chief, Satan himself. The father-of-lies likes nothing more than to send more deluded, often poorly educated, folk on a spiritual wild goose chase ending in Hell.

I also include a chapter on one of the world's most popular false belief systems: global (non) warming, which has rapidly become a cult in its own right, one which stands no correction and is promoted with neo-religious fervour. Well, I have tried to correct it!

Psychics, spiritism and New Age beliefs are everywhere in the west and again, I have felt it necessary to include a warning chapter. Many are sucked into the occult via "psychic advice" lines, psychic television shows and public tours by so-called mediums. Avoid them: if they are in touch with anyone, it is demons — fallen angels.

We conclude with a brief look at other popular myths, misunderstandings, false religions and wrong-headed semi-religious ideas. These are times of deception, the hallmark of the end times. Become forewarned, forearmed with the facts and be like the noble Bereans. Search the scriptures daily to see if these things are true or false. We hope our book helps point you in the right direction, the direction of the one true faith, the one true Messiah, the once and coming king, the Lord Jesus Christ.

The cults are thick on the ground, which is a sign of the times pointing to the soon return of our Lord. Some marks of a cult:

- Denial of the deity of the Lord Jesus Christ / the Trinity / the atoning death, burial and resurrection of the Lord Jesus.
- The Bible plus. They add their book or books or, in the case of the Catholics, tradition, to the Bible — and their books or their traditions take precedence over God's Word.
- They preach a different gospel. Salvation is not through faith in Christ alone, and salvation is not assured.
- They claim to be the one true church or faith or group; salvation is not through faith alone, but through *them* alone.
- They have a strong leader or leaders who cannot be challenged.
- There may be visions of supernatural beings, and these beings are not tested by Bible standards; what they say is just accepted as from God.
- They claim to have true prophets who speak direct revelation from God, so no one is allowed to question them.
- They do not repent when their prophecies fail; they cover it all up or find some excuse.
- There is often involvement with the occult in some way, e.g. divination through staring at or through objects until some "revelation" comes; or meditating in an unbiblical way by blanking out their mind, waiting for something to be revealed (this is a trance state when one is open to demonic influence).
- Immorality among the leadership at some stage, since false doctrine inevitably leads to immorality. In the case of the Catholic Church, we have seen it in an explosion of bad publicity, and the known cases of paedophilia may well be just the tip of the iceberg.
- Iron control of members, who are never allowed to think for themselves.
- Fear of losing your salvation if you leave the cult.

Roll of Dishonor. A roll call of some of the false prophets. There is no questioning them, for their pronouncements come from "god".

- Joseph Smith — Mormons (followed by Brigham Young). Young left $2 million when he died.)
- Ellen G. White — Seventh Day Adventists.
- Baha'u'llah — Bahai religion (Islam minus the violence).
- Pope — considered to speak infallibly, with the full authority of God, when making official *ex cathedra* pronouncements to the Roman Catholic Church.
- Buddha — Buddhism.
- Mohammed — Islam.
- Many men and women on religious TV claim to be prophets — Word of Faith movement.

The test of a true prophet: "When a prophet speaketh in the name of the Lord, if the thing follow not, nor come to pass, that is the thing which the Lord hath not spoken, but the prophet hath spoken it presumptuously: thou shalt not be afraid of him." Deuteronomy 18:22

"In the latter times some shall depart from the faith, giving heed to seducing spirits, and doctrines of devils; speaking lies in hypocrisy, having their conscience seared with a hot iron..." 1 Timothy 4:1, 2

"Evil men and seducers shall wax worse and worse, deceiving, and being deceived." 2 Timothy 3:13

Chapter 1

The Watchmen on The Wall
by Alan Franklin

"For thus hath the Lord said unto me, Go, set a watchman, let him declare what he seeth."

Isaiah 21:6

We live in interesting times. If you are not a saved Christian they are terrifying times — or soon will be. Israel, God's chosen nation, is being backed into a corner by a sinister alliance of world powers. In the background is the EU superstate and the man who will become Antichrist may already be there in the wings, awaiting his debut on the world stage. For the time is rapidly approaching when the EU, the revived Roman Empire, will run the world with Antichrist at its head. Already America is falling from its pre-eminent role in the world, undermined by financial excess, indebtedness, and, worst of all, spiritual promiscuity and an abandonment of the state of Israel.

The rapture of the real church is near, for this will happen before the coming seven year tribulation period, the worst time in the history of the world, the years the Bible refers to as "the time of Jacob's troubles." We are in the scenario laid out in Matthew 24, when we are warned of the state of the world in the end times.

As the world's finances teeter and crash, global solutions are increasingly propounded as the way forward, coupled with global "spirituality." Former British Prime Minister Tony Blair, now a Middle East "peace envoy", has said he wants to unite religions. He declared on May 29, 2008: "I'll dedicate the rest of my life to uniting the world's religions… faith is part of our future and faith and the values it brings with it are an essential part of making globalization work." But faith in what, exactly? Faith in "Mother Earth"? Faith in faith? The world abounds in false faith and we will be exposing much of it in this book.

The green religion and mother earth fantasies are a major part of our education process, also known as brainwashing. Ask any western child what the biggest dangers in the world are and he or she might well say something like: global warming and religious fundamentalism. You can be a fundamentalist greenie and allow no alternative views — debate about global non-warming, for example — to be broadcast or printed. But woe betide anyone who holds that the words of the Bible are literally true, for that makes us — and Pat and I believe that the Bible is God's book — dangerous extremists.

There has been a deliberate blurring of the differences — total, 100 per cent diametrically opposed differences, between fundamentalist Muslims, whose aim is to kill people and wipe all opposition off the face of the earth, and committed fundamentalist Christians, who follow the example of the Lord Jesus and seek to teach people that He is the only way to heaven and that we must follow God's laws of morality and sexuality as laid out in the Bible — the Maker's handbook. Not a popular concept among the trendy bishops and homosexual priests who pollute many of the world's pulpits, at least in the west. Here's Tony Blair again, working to change the thinking of Christians in relation to homosexuality. Ruth Gledhill, religious correspondent of *The Times* (of London) quotes Blair as follows: "In my Faith Foundation I have a lot of links with some of the evangelical groups in the US and elsewhere and actually I think there is a generational shift that is happening there. If you talk to the older generation, you will still get parts of the Bible quoted. But if you talk to the younger generation of evangelicals, this is something they wish to be out of, at least in terms of having their position confined to being anti gay."

Blair's right-hand man was for years Peter Mandelson,[1] an openly homosexual politician who went on to be Britain's commissioner at the European Union, where he was in charge of trade. Blair and those he influences seem to be trying to reinvent the Bible, ignoring the bits they don't agree with, leaving a pale, gutted faith that real Bible-believers will not recognize. There will be no place for absolutes in the coming New World Order, the only sin then being that it is wrong to be judgmental. That mindless tolerance will not extend to true Christians — the remnant church — who will be judged harshly!

---

[1] Now he is "Lord" Mandelson, a blasphemous and disgraceful title.

No wonder people are turning in huge numbers to cults and isms. These tend to know what they believe in, even if it is a load of old tosh, demonstrably so in every case.

Cults and isms — and the biggest ones are Catholicism and Islam — invariably speak with authority and are not racked with doubts, as many denominational church leaders often seem to be. If the trumpet sounds an uncertain note, who will follow it? That's the way to lose the battle for souls. People are looking for figures of authority in these troubled times and Satan's deceivers are good at their work, as Dr. Goebbels was. Speak out a big lie often enough and billions believe. You can fool most of the world most of the time.

The only free medium where the truth can be told, mixed up with a lot of misinformation, is the web. This too is under imminent threat, as the powers-that-be aim is bring it into politically-correct line, just like all the rest of the media. Christian talk radio, preachers' pulpits, truthful websites like our own, thefreepressonline.co.uk, are all likely to come under intense pressure to toe the politically correct line or close down.

Here comes the New World Order, global religion, global government and soon, emerging from the shadows, the man of sin himself, Antichrist, running the world and dancing to Satan's tune. Be warned, be watchful, be like the noble Bereans and search the scriptures daily. These are times of great deception, inside and outside the church.

The world has turned aside from the truth and instead believes a lie and, if they follow so-called Christian preachers at all, follow those who teach what their itching ears want to hear. They follow a god of wealth and goodies, but name it and claim it ministries will have a hard time delivering their happiness gospels and wealth doctrines as the world collapses into the Greater Depression I have been forecasting since 2006.

Christians in the west could be accused of fighting a losing cause, for the world is not getting better — quite the reverse. Pornography, abortion, crime and violence are all increasing, yet there are no moral absolutes taught in schools. Everything is relative — my truth is no better than your truth. Or so our rulers would have you believe.

The result is that socially, America, Britain and many other countries are falling apart and around 50 per cent of live births in the UK are now to single parents. Britain is now post Christian and fast becoming pagan. Among 14 countries analyzed in a report by America's National Center for Health Statistics, 40 per cent of America's babies were born to unmarried mothers in 2007, up from 18 per cent in 1980.

Countries with a higher proportion of births to unmarried mothers include Iceland, Sweden, Norway, France, Denmark and Britain; countries with a lower percentage than the USA include Ireland, Germany, Canada, Spain, Italy and Japan. Societies where children are not raised in stable homes are destined to rapidly fall apart, even without war.

The world is on red alert for the next major war, which could come at any time. North Korea is the ninth country to announce it has the atomic bomb. Israel is the tenth, although it has never admitted this. Sooner or later, these weapons will be used. We know Damascus will be destroyed overnight, for example.[2]

So are we wasting our time? Should we all go home and watch television, or wash the car? Or should we be anticipating the most exciting time in 2000 years, the second coming of Jesus Christ? Don't allow the bad things happening to rob you of the joy of this anticipation. The Bible says we are to yearn for the return of the Lord.[3] Most of the church today is yawning…

Christians are not called to "win". We are not to fight crusades — at least, not with armies. In fact, in many ways we will seem to lose the battle. The world is set to get a lot worse, very soon. Satan is the ruler of this world and will continue to be until our Lord returns, when Satan will be bound for 1000 years.[4] Satan has a master plan — but God has THE master plan. Satan is the ultimate loser, but he seems to win for a while. If he tries to remind us of our past we can always remind him of his future[5] — no wonder he tries to stifle the study of prophecy! We cannot control Satan; as Christians our job is to stand for righteousness. Until our rapture or death, we have to spread the word, to speak out on behalf of God's principles. For many it will be costly.

As preacher Jacob Prasch, a member of our fellowship, has said — some will be saved off the rocks. Matthew 5, verses 10 to 14, part of the Sermon on the Mount, says: "Blessed are they which are persecuted for righteousness' sake, for theirs is the kingdom of heaven. Blessed are ye when men shall revile you, and persecute you, and say all manner of evil against you falsely, for My sake. Rejoice and be exceeding glad: for great is your reward in heaven: for so persecuted they the prophets which were before you.

"Ye are the salt of the earth: but if the salt has lost its savour, wherewith shall it be salted? It is thenceforth good for nothing, but to be cast out and to be trodden under foot of men.

---

[2] Isaiah Chapter 17.
[3] 2 Timothy 4:7, 8; Titus 2:13.
[4] Revelation 20:1–3.
[5] Satan's ultimate future is in the Lake of Fire. Revelation. Chapter 20.

Ye are the light of the world. A city that is set on a hill cannot be hid."

Watchmen were set on high places to warn of pending danger. The Lord has watchmen doing the same today — the SWRC, the South West Radio Church based in Oklahoma City and broadcasting round America and the world, has as its motto the watchman on the wall. Ezekiel 33 tells of the watchman's role from verse two onwards.

The people are told to appoint a watchman whose job is to blow the trumpet when danger looms. Those who do not heed the watchman's warning have their blood on their own heads. Conversely, if the watchman sees danger, but doesn't alert the people, he will pay with his blood. These are serious matters for serious times; times when the world would rather watch sport and soap operas when the greatest story never told is unfolding before their lidded eyes. Be warned, be wary; this book is your watchman's call! Once you know the truth it becomes your responsibility as well.

Israel is a country that needs watchmen today. Israelis, for the most part, think that it is their own brilliance and courage that has protected them since 1948, winning wars they had no right to win — or seemingly no chance of winning. Even military analysts have said that there is no way some of the battles could have been won by any rational expectation. Israel is something special.

Here is a message our daughter Annie e-mailed to us from her home in northern Israel:

"We had our first rain in the night. Boy, did it rain! Now it is beautifully clear and sunny with a slightly cool breeze. I'm hoping the rain breaks the worst of the heat.

Usually the rains come around the time of the Feast of Tabernacles and today was the day after the end of the feast. An old lady here was telling me through the hot summer months and hamsins (a few days of hot desert winds), 'At Tabernacles there'll be a deluge!' She was right. You can't help but think of the spiritual significance — that Tabernacles is the feast that marks the setting up of the Millennial Kingdom, when the Holy Spirit will be given to all the nation of Israel, who will all be believers."

Added Annie: "Before that is the long summer with no rain whatsoever, until a couple of small showers precede the first rain, but are not considered the first rain because there's not enough rain. I guess those little showers are the period we're in now.

"The fact that Israel is dependent on the rains is also interesting. Egypt is not dependent upon rain, for example, but lives off the resources of the Nile delta, which only runs low in extreme conditions. That's why Abraham and Isaac both would go down to Egypt when there was drought in Israel. God wants to make sure that Israel stays dependent upon Him and I believe this is His way with believers also. He never wants us to feel that we're self sufficient."

Israel is the major subject of the Bible, yet few who live there today really know its author. Only when all else fails and they face extinction at the final battle for Jerusalem will a remnant — one-third of the Jews — turn to God, when they embrace the Son of God who comes to rescue them. It takes the Tribulation to soften their hearts. My point is, only by repentance and trusting in Jesus Christ for forgiveness of sin can anyone — Jews or Gentiles — be saved by grace. It is not something the church can engineer. Neither can the church save the world. We can, however, warn the world. This is what we will do in this book, for these end times are times of great deception, just as Jude and others warned would be the case.

If ever two countries needed a watchman's warning, they are America and Britain, going giggling to their graves as nations. Just as with sin-ridden Israel, there is a spiritual cause for all our troubles, as London becomes Londonistan, and 27 European countries give up their sovereignty to the EU superstate, — the rising revived Roman Empire from which will emerge Antichrist, heading up the coming one world government. God has given us over to our evil desires to see how we like the end results.

We as watchmen are here to please God, not to please people. To be a light in the gloom, to tell people they do not need to choose destruction. All round the world Christians are being martyred in ever increasing numbers as the world's hatred turns against real Christianity. Christians are under persecution in many parts of the world, with believers imprisoned and pastors killed. In ALL Islamic countries, becoming a Christian is a life threatening experience. Yet many in these countries are secretly becoming believers, facing death the moment their secret is out. They are pleasing God, not men. They are saving their souls when all around them are losing theirs.

Yet all over the western world, millions of cars are purpose driven into church car parks every Sunday. A quarter of a million pastors listen to Rick Warren's purpose driven messages and adapt them for their own flocks. Warren's books, financed by Rupert Murdoch's organisation, sell in tens of millions. Surely this is the church victorious? Turn on the religious channels and you sometimes see churches with tens of thousands of members. In one mega-church we hear there is a two year wait for an appointment with the pastor! In America they buy millions of books in order to become Purpose Driven, enriching Murdoch, owner of the sleazy *Sun* newspaper in Britain and the even sleazier *News of the World*, and also one of the world's leading Bible publishers with Zondervan. If the millions in the mega-churches were hearing the true gospel, our societies, in Britain and America, would not be fast gurgling down the plughole. So why is it happening?

Deception is the answer — the huge spiritual problem of the end times. Many churches are Laodicean — lukewarm. There is a great falling away from biblical truth. Jesus said: "Take heed that no man deceive you. For many shall come IN MY NAME..." In His name! Matthew 24:4, 5. Take heed, folks! Paul warns in 1 Timothy 4:1: "In the latter times some shall depart from the faith, giving heed to seducing spirits..." The very word "fundamental" has acquired a bad reputation, when all it means when applied to Christians is that you believe the fundamental truths of the Bible. Many ministers and bishops deny the most foundational truths of our faith — the virgin birth, the atoning death and the resurrection of Christ.

Jude foresaw all this. He wanted to write about salvation but instead commented, verse 3 and 4: "I felt the necessity to write to you appealing that you contend earnestly for the faith which was once for all delivered to the saints. For certain persons have crept in unnoticed, those who were long beforehand marked out for this condemnation, ungodly persons who turn the grace of our God into licentiousness and deny our only master and Lord, Jesus Christ."

Jude goes on to warn against homosexuality, verse 7: "Even as Sodom and Gomorrah and the cities about them in like manner, giving themselves over to fornication, and going after strange flesh, are set forth as an example, suffering the vengeance of eternal fire."

Eternal fire is what awaits every unrepentant homosexual, so why are churches today ordaining homosexual priests or saying homosexuality is just another lifestyle? That's not how God sees it. When we flew to Israel we went over the site of Sodom, marked on the plane's map. British Airways are not known as fundamentalists, but there it was — the site of the city destroyed by sin. In the same way New Orleans was judged, and San Francisco will be.

Yet the head of the Anglican church in America, Bishop Katherine Jefferts Schori, is a woman. A deceived woman. She favored the ordination of Bishop Gene Robinson, the first openly homosexual bishop.

She says sodomy is "a given characteristic, not chosen." This is untrue and no scientific study has ever backed this up. Notice the word *sin* is never used. Says Bishop Kate, when asked about how homosexuality is declared a sin in the Bible: "The Bible was written in a very different historical context by people asking different questions." Please note: You cannot throw out the bits of the Bible you do not like or which have become unfashionable.

The same convocation that elected Bishop Schori saw delegates pass a resolution expressing "regret" for consecrating Robinson. Next day they voted to continue consecrating homosexual bishops. A day later, they reversed themselves again and called on the church to avoid consecrating additional gay bishops. One writer observed: "Apparently they are so wishy washy that they are even wishy washy about their wishy-washiness." That's how the world sees the church. In England the black robed ones of the Church of England agonise about whether God is male, as do Methodists and others in America. The Bible always addresses the Father as male.

Of course, if Bishop Kate took time out from campaigning on social issues and pushing the feminist agenda to read the Bible, she might find a few scriptures not to her liking. She thinks women can do anything men can do, but the Bible says:

"Let the woman learn in silence with all subjection. I suffer not a woman to teach, nor to usurp authority over the man, but to be in silence."   1 Timothy 2:11, 12

As Pat writes in our book, *Goodbye America, Goodbye Britain*: "These scriptures teach that women are not to have a public leadership ministry in the church, but there is still plenty we can do. Jesus loves us and a woman (Mary Magdalene) was privileged to be the first person on earth to see Him after He rose from the dead. Mary was on a mission of mercy, to take care of a practical need, and what divine favor she found! There certainly is scope for merciful acts today."

As well as false doctrines, there are false "Christs" deceiving many *(Matthew 24:5)*. The Greek word "Christ" means "anointed one." Jesus is the anointed one, the true Christ, the only one to fulfill the Old Testament prophecies of Israel's Messiah. He alone can baptize with the Holy Spirit. Yet there are men today standing on platforms in churches shouting: "I have the anointing!" No they do not. Only Jesus has the anointing. The closer we get to the Lord's return, the more false "Christs" will come, and many foolish people will follow them. Do not listen to those who claim to perform miracle healings or to "take authority" over the weather. Such men are deceived.

As new believers in the 1980s we soon got enmeshed in the Kingdom Now philosophy that is everywhere in false churches. We were misled into thinking we could "claim" things for Christ. In my stupidity I once walked round a newspaper plant, "claiming" it. I didn't get it, and I don't think any of the many publications printed there ever carried the good news of the gospel.

"We're gonna take this town (nation, planet) for Jesus Christ," say these deceived souls. Rick Warren says he will mobilise a million Christians to do just that. Funny, that's not what Jesus said. This Kingdom Now teaching has deceived many people, who are wasting good prayer time "claiming" their towns for Christ and marching through areas to "break Satan's strongholds". We are not going to "take" any territory for the Lord Jesus. It's all His anyway. We are not going to "bind" Satan or any other evil spirits over our towns. That is not in our power to do. Paul didn't do that in the pagan towns. Ever since marches for Jesus started the world has become worse and worse. We are not going to "bring the kingdom in."

The Lord Jesus will do that with no help from us, after he destroys His enemies gathered in Israel. Only He acts, His enemies are killed by the words from His mouth.[6] In the meantime, far from "taking" any towns, we will be hated and persecuted, just as He forewarned us in John 15.[7] And, as evil waxes worse and worse, the professing church will continue deeper and deeper into apostasy, just as is happening today. It gets worse, not better, to the point where Jesus asks in Luke 18:8, "Nevertheless when the Son of man cometh, shall he find faith on the earth?" The implied answer is: "No, He will find precious little faith on the earth." Just like now.

"The time will come when they will not endure sound doctrine; but after their own lusts shall they heap to themselves teachers, having itching ears."[8] Those teaching simple Bible truths are not popular; their books sell in hundreds, not millions! People mostly want "easy believism."

"Just claim your healing!" Another great myth of what passes for Christianity today. So how come so many Christians are sick and dying — why are we not clearing the wards of our hospitals? Just name it

---

[6] Revelation 19:21.
[7] "If they have persecuted me, they will also persecute you..." John 15:20.
[8] 2 Timothy 4:3, 4.

and claim it? Really? As Dr. J. Vernon McGee says, yes, healing is in the atonement, as are all our blessings, but we do not possess the fullness of the blessings yet. For example, Paul tells us in Ephesians 2:6 that we are seated with Christ in heavenly places — but this is prophetic; we are not there yet. We also have eternal life — but for now, life is a struggle down here on earth. Yes, Jesus won the victory at the cross, but many of our blessings are future.

The hyper-charismatics would almost have you feeling guilty for being ill. What nonsense. The great apostle Paul was ill. He did not "claim his healing" as many try to do today. He says in Galatians 4:13–14: "…ye know how through infirmity of the flesh I preached the gospel unto you at the first." He adds that although his illness was a trial to them, they nevertheless received him as an angel of God, as Christ Jesus Himself.

His fellow workers also were stricken with sickness. "For indeed he (Epaphroditus) was sick nigh unto death, but God had mercy on him; and not on him only, but on me also, lest I should have sorrow upon sorrow."[9] Notice that God had mercy on Epaphroditus; it was not his right to be healed, but a favor from the Lord.

"Trophimus have I left in Miletum sick."[10] Paul, who worked so many miracles, did not heal Trophimus. If only Benny Hinn had been around then…

We do not need fables and follies, we need godly leadership. We must concentrate on saving souls rather than healing minds, with so-called Christian "psychology." We need the faith in God that sent missionaries round the world and built Britain and then America into the greatest nations on earth, something astonishing for a nation of Britain's size, just as it is astonishing for Israel to be so strong today.

A nation without true faith — not faith in faith, but faith in Jesus — cannot stand for long. God judges nations in many ways and Britain has now lost its sovereignty, with America about to follow suit, while most people are too lazy and ill informed to have noticed. We must start making judgements, for the claim that tolerance must be our guideline for life is itself an intolerant statement.

God honors nations that honor Him, rather than question all that He has set out in His book — the Maker's handbook, the book that guides us through life to everlasting life. Nations need conviction so that storms do not shake them and our democracy is failing as we have turned to man

---

[9] Philippians 2:27.
[10] 2 Timothy 4:20.

from God and our freedoms are following the Bible out of the door.

The more we break His rules, the more rules the godless governments impose, until soon, all freedom has gone. We are almost at that point in Europe, just awaiting a word from Brussels to act against evangelical Christians. A Baptist mother in Germany was arrested at gunpoint for teaching her children at home. The family had to flee to Austria. The rule was brought in by Hitler, who wanted state control over pupils' minds — just like today.

John the Baptist cried: "Behold the Lamb of God which taketh away the sin of the world!"[11] True justice and mercy will occur when the Lamb returns as a conquering lion — and the Hebrew prophets used this image to symbolize the Second Advent. The Messiah was pictured as a roaring lion who comes to pour out the wrath of God on those who have rejected the Lord's grace, mercy and love. "The Lord shall roar from on high and utter His voice from His holy habitation; He shall mightily roar upon His habitation; He shall give a shout, as they that tread the grapes, against all the inhabitants of the earth."[12] Chapter ten of Revelation shows Jesus at His second coming, portrayed as a mighty angel who returns to earth with the scroll open in His hand. He comes to claim the earth for His saints — us — who will rule with Him. Using Old Testament imagery, the passage says He will cry out "with a loud voice, as when a lion roareth."

Woe to the fallen world. It has ignored God's ultimatum and faces His wrath. But one day soon, every knee will bow. Meanwhile, the deceivers are here. Their time is short and in the following pages we expose them.

Maranatha — come, Lord Jesus.

---

[11] John 1:29 and 36.
[12] Jeremiah 25:30.

Chapter 2

My Story
by Pat Franklin

When the Savior reached down for me
He had to reach way down for me
I was lost and alone without God or His Son
When He reached down His Hand for me...

I was raised as a Catholic in the USA and went to Catholic schools in St Louis, Missouri, until the age of 18. In college, at the age of 19, I completely lost my faith, becoming an agnostic (someone who says it is impossible to know whether or not God exists). Since I no longer tried to please God, I became a liberal, with only contempt for Christianity. And since God was pushed out of my life, His rules went too, and I was a very sinful person.

After my last year of college in 1967, I travelled to England. Like the prodigal, I went to a far country. I hoped to find a teaching job, but somehow fell into journalism instead.

Then, in 1981, I had an encounter with God. I was 36 when He entered my life in a dramatic fashion. By then I was married and living with my British husband, Alan, and our 3-year-old son Daniel, in the town of Alton, Hampshire. Alan and I ran our own newspaper and I had signed up our son for the playgroup at the local evangelical church. Unknown to me, the pastor (who is no longer at that church) and others there were praying for us. In fact the pastor had prayed one night asking God to show him someone whose heart was ready, so that he could pray for them, and he said: "Lord, please let them use the words 'born again' so that I know who to pray for." Not many people would ever use those words — certainly not me!

The next morning was playgroup day at the church hall and although the pastor never normally came in, that day he did. He went round speaking briefly to each of the mothers, and when he got to me and introduced himself, I asked: "Is your church one of those that believe in being born again?" I asked this because I had just received a letter from my sister Carol in America, saying she had been born again! The pastor told me much later that as soon as I used those words, he knew I was the one he should pray for. That was in October, 1980. Three months later, in January, 1981, I was converted to faith in the Lord Jesus Christ.

My conversion came about in an odd way. In those days we read a daily newspaper, which was carrying a series of articles about a young woman who died of skin cancer. She had noticed a small black spot on her body and it was not long before she was dying. The articles gripped me; her death was so sad. Then one morning in the shower, I noticed there was a small black spot on my skin too. Fear hit me like a cold wave. If I died of cancer, who would ever love our little boy as much as I did? That was the first thought in my mind. The second thought was to pray. Pray? Me, the staunch liberal who despised Christianity? Yes, pray. As they say about wars — there are no atheists (or agnostics) on the battlefield. When the chips are down, you pray, or else you are a fool. Actually, I was a fool, but not that big a fool.

So it was that I prayed to the God I had denied. My prayer was this: "If You will let this not be cancer, I will make one last effort to find out if You exist." This prayer strikes me as dangerously impertinent now, but, true to His loving and merciful nature, the Lord had patience with me.

I went to my doctor, who said she did not think the black spot was cancer, but to put my mind at rest, she said I should go and see a skin specialist in the town of Winchester. This I did. The specialist took one look and said it was definitely not cancer and I could make an appointment to have the black spot removed.

It felt like I was walking on air as I left his office, as though I had been reprieved, but the thought was in my mind that now I had to keep my part of the bargain, to try to find out if God really existed. I decided then and there that I would read the New Testament all the way through, something I had never done.

And since I was in the beautiful town of Winchester, I took the opportunity to visit the famous old cathedral. It was my favorite place to take American visitors, since it was free (no longer!), but that day was different. I didn't stroll around the ancient building like the tourists were doing, but sat down in one of the wooden chairs, each of which contained books in racks. I picked up a book from the chair in front of me and opened it. As I read the words on the page, those same words came down through the high roof of that cathedral and shot straight into my brain. Don't ask me how or why; I have no idea — I just know that that is exactly what happened. The words were these:

"Except a man be born again, he cannot see the kingdom of God."   John 3:3

I sat there stunned. I was no longer an agnostic. I knew for certain that God existed and that He had just spoken to me — in the pages of a book and through the roof of a cathedral.

Somehow I knew there was something else in the book. I read on, and soon came to it. Once again, the words came through the roof and went straight into my brain. The words were:

"Go ye therefore, and teach all nations, baptizing them in the name of the Father, and of the Son, and of the Holy Ghost: teaching them to observe all things whatsoever I have commanded you..."   Matthew 28:19

I looked round to see if any of the tourists had heard or noticed anything, but they were just casually strolling around as before. I understood that God had just told me that I was supposed to go somewhere and tell people something, but what? I had no idea. And the first statement, about being "born again", was a complete mystery to me. What in the world did it mean? I didn't have a clue.

My youngest sister Carol had written a letter to me three months earlier, going on and on for several pages about being born again. She claimed that she had become a Christian and her life was completely changed. I had not understood one word of her letter, but here it was again — the words "born again" — and this time it had come from God through the roof of a great cathedral.

My heart was already beginning to open in love towards the God I had rejected for so long. I left Winchester Cathedral, no longer walking on air, but something more akin to walking on eggs. Something amazing, something marvellous, was happening, something I could not begin to understand.

That night I put our son to bed at 8 pm as usual, but instead of turning the TV on, I got the Bible down off the shelf. It was a King James Bible, which had been given to my husband, Alan, when he finished secondary school in England in 1960. Every teenager then got one. On the inside was an inscription: "The Surrey Education Committee presents you with this Book, the most valuable thing this world affords, desiring that you use it whilst at school and retain it when you leave. Herein is wisdom which will lead you to all truth, provide comfort and guidance and teach you the whole duty of man. March, 1960."

No one had ever read that Bible. Alan had suggested getting rid of it on various occasions, but I had hung on to it just because I like books. That night I opened it to the gospel of Matthew, Chapter 1, and read: ***"The book of the generation of Jesus Christ, the son of David, the son of Abraham,"*** tracing some of the actual family line[1] of the Lord Jesus from the time of Abraham. I, who had sneered at God for many years, suddenly knew without any doubt whatsoever that every word was true and accurate, that this book was like no other book in the world, that this was God's very own book.

Every evening I read a bit further, and was constantly surprised. In my years as a liberal, I had devised explanations for all the miracles, but now I realised that Jesus really had done all the wondrous miracles ascribed to Him, that He was indescribably gentle and kind and yet forceful and strong — all powerful and yet perfectly meek. I began to admire Him and love Him with all my heart.

The horrible part was that I could see I had completely blown it in my life and totally failed to live the way the Lord Jesus would have wanted. I was in an agony of mind, thinking of how I had offended Him over the course of many years. Nothing could be changed; the past was unalterable; I was completely lost and richly deserved to go to hell, the terrible place which Jesus warned of in the gospels.

The days went by and every evening I read a bit more. By the time I had read through the gospels of Matthew and Mark and got to about the middle of Luke, I was in real distress. One evening, I could stand it no longer. I went upstairs to the bedroom and fell to my knees in tears, saying: "Oh Lord Jesus, I see now that Your book is true, that You really are the Son of God; that You really did all those miracles, and died on the cross. I have done so many things wrong. Could You ever forgive me?" I thought through my whole life and mentally listed every single sin I could remember. I begged the Lord to forgive me and to make me one of His people. I told Him He could have everything I possessed and every minute of my time from then on.

Although I did not realise it then, that was the turning point of my

---

[1] I learned later that the genealogy in Matthew does not list every ancestor, but certain ones for certain reasons. His gospel is directed mainly at the Jewish people and points up the fact of our Lord's Jewish ancestry and specifically that His birth fulfils prophecies relating to the long-awaited Jewish Messiah — son of Abraham, tribe of Judah, descendent of King David, with a legal right to the throne of Israel.

life. The moment I whispered out that prayer on my knees in the privacy
of my bedroom, I was born again of the Holy Spirit and forgiven of all
my sins. I did not know this at the time. In fact, I didn't think the Lord
Jesus would hear any prayer coming from a bad person like me. All I
knew was that I believed absolutely, and there was no turning back,
because I had finally found the truth, and I was going to follow the Lord
Jesus, even if He rejected me.

I continued reading the Bible every day, and one day Alan said: "You
know, Pat, if you want to become a Christian, I wouldn't stand in your
way." I answered weakly: "I think I might be one already."

A week or so later I told a Christian lady I knew at the church playgroup, Anne Heath[2], about the prayer I had prayed, and that I had asked
the Lord to make me one of His people, but that I didn't think He would
ever want me. She said: "Pat, that was all He was waiting for!" Anne
made an appointment to meet me and go through some scriptures. Together we looked them up and, as we read some of the marvellous salvation promises, a smile grew bigger and bigger on my face as I realised
what had happened to me.

The Bible verses we looked up included some of these:

"No one is good except God alone."   Luke 18:9

(That was very comforting to me; I wasn't the only rotten sinner;
everyone was in the same sinking boat!)

**"The Son of Man has come to seek and to save that which was
lost."**   Luke 18:10

**"It is not those who are well who need a physician, but those
who are sick. I have not come to call the righteous, but sinners to repentance."**   Luke 5:32

**"If we confess our sins, He is faithful and righteous to forgive
us our sins and to cleanse us from all unrighteousness."**
                                                            1 John 1: 9

"Truly, truly, I say to you, he who believes has eternal life."
                                                            John 6:47

(How could this be? I had won eternal life simply by believing the
Bible! I was so happy…)

**"I am the resurrection and the life; he who believes in Me will
live, even if he dies."**   John 11:25

---

[2] Anne Heath is now a missionary in Ghana.

(It was a miracle! I was going to heaven, guaranteed, despite my sinful life. I was saved!)

"He who has believed and has been baptized shall be saved; but he who has disbelieved shall be condemned."

Mark 16:16

"Believe in the Lord Jesus and you will be saved,..."

Acts 16:31

"For by grace you have been saved through faith; and that not of yourselves, it is the gift of God, not as a result of works, so that no one may boast." Ephesians 2:8–9

"If a man loves me, he will keep my word; and my Father will love him, and we will come unto him and make our abode with him." John 14:23

(That is what had happened; that is why I was completely different inside ever since the night I prayed.)

"Therefore there is now no condemnation for those who are in Christ Jesus." Romans 8:1

(My sins were gone!)

"Therefore if anyone is in Christ, he is a new creature; the old things passed away; behold, new things have come."

2 Corinthians 5:17

"Do you not know that you are a temple of God and that the Spirit of God dwells in you? 1 Corinthians 3:16

"...we are the temple of the living God..." 2 Corinthians 6:16

As we looked up the scriptures together, I realised that I had been born again. That strange term "born again" which I hadn't been able to understand — it meant I had been spiritually born. Before that, I had been spiritually dead; the Bible calls it "dead in trespasses and sins." I was *physically* born when my mother gave birth. I was *spiritually* born, meaning my spirit came to life, when I believed in the Lord Jesus after reading the Bible. At that moment the Holy Spirit came to live inside me, indeed He personally sealed me as a kind of down payment of eternal life.[3]

---

[3] "For by one Spirit are we all baptized into one body, whether we be Jews or Gentiles, whether we be bond or free; and have been all made to drink into one Spirit." 1 Corinthians 12:13.
"Now if any man have not the Spirit of Christ, he is none of his." Romans 8:9/

How I thank the Lord for His incredible plan of salvation and His unchangeable character. How can Someone so powerful be so kind and merciful? That is the greatest mystery of all. Why would He ever want anything to do with a sinner like me, deserving only of His judgement? His love is inexplicable. **"God so loved the world that he gave his only-begotten Son…"** John 3:16. How I thank Him for His mercy on me. In the words of the old hymn:

I know not why God's wondrous grace to me He hath made known
Nor why, unworthy, Christ in love redeemed me for His own
But I know whom I have believed, and am persuaded that He is able
To keep that which I've committed unto Him against that day.

After I was born again in 1981, as a "new creature" in Christ, I began studying the Bible, have done so ever since and hope I will never stop, since I do not know it nearly as well as I should. Does this mean that I was suddenly a wonderful, perfect person? I wish! No, it was the beginning of my walk through the rest of life attempting to follow the Lord and please Him, but failing so often, again and again needing His mercy and grace, which He never fails to give.

You too can become born again as a "new creation" and begin a new life in Christ. The Lord Jesus wants you to come to Him in repentance and faith, for He says to all readers of this book:

"Come to me, all ye that labour and are heavy laden, and I will give you rest. Take my yoke upon you and learn of me, for I am meek and lowly in heart, and ye shall find rest unto your souls. For my yoke is easy and my burden is light."
Matthew 11: 28–30

This is so true. His yoke really is easy. If He wants you to do something, He makes it do-able, because He is yoked in there with you and He has done the hardest part already at the cross. You simply walk along with Him, following the direction He chooses for you, and when you hit an uphill, difficult bit, you just keep on, you don't give up. Seek His forgiveness and give Him your heart today, dear reader; why would you want to go your own sinful, miserable way, when you can walk with God?

One woman said to me: "I could never become a Christian because I have cancer and to believe now would just make me a hypocrite." Nonsense! *Now* is the day of salvation, whether you are in perfect health or sitting in the doctor's office scared half to death. Don't worry about being a hypocrite. Worry instead about spending all of eternity in the fires of hell. Worry about missing out on what God has on offer for you and then kicking yourself for the next thousand billion years. Satan will feed you any old lie to get you to reject Jesus. Do not fall for his tricks. Look to the Savior, and put your trust in the One who loves you. Stop listening to Satan, who hates you and plots your destruction.

Read through those scriptures listed earlier in this chapter and pray with all your heart for the Lord to forgive you and make you one of His people. He will do it for you, just as He did it for me. He is no respecter of persons. If you are the Queen of England or the person who cleans the toilets — He will hear your prayer and give you a new life. If you have lived a fairly straightforward, mostly moral life or have been an out and out sinner — whatever your past might be — you are in desperate need of the Savior, just as I was. He will put you on that narrow way which leads to heaven, with a guaranteed place just for you, a place He has gone to prepare. Why wait? Right now is a good time to be born again! Today is the day of salvation.

I want to say something about the experience in Winchester Cathedral. When I tell other Christians my testimony, sometimes they say: "Wow, I wish something dramatic like that would happen to me." I tell them not to be so silly, that their own testimony is every bit as precious. The dramatic experience did not save me; I was still a sinner bound for hell. The absolutely vital thing came later — reading the words of truth in the Bible, coming to believe them and praying to the Lord for forgiveness.

These days people are too easily awed by experiences. Peter, James and John had the ultimate experience of being on the mountaintop with Jesus when God's glory was revealed. Did Peter trade on that for the rest of his life? No. Even though he had heard the voice of God the Father speaking from a cloud, he knew scripture was far more important than even that awesome experience. He said:

"We have also a more sure word of prophecy whereunto ye do well that ye take heed, as unto a light that shineth in a dark place..." 1 Peter 1:19

In other words — that "more sure word of prophecy" is the Bible, the Scriptures, God's Word to mankind, His lamp for our feet, His light for our path. The stuff that sounds so exciting — visions, dreams, voices, signs, wonders — all can be counterfeited, all can be used to deceive us. The only certain body of truth in this world is in God's book.

An elderly man I knew died. He was "a nice man" who was quite helpful to his neighbours. I don't know of anything wrong he ever did, but I know that, like every other human being, he was not good enough to face Almighty God on his own merits. I had tried to tell this man of the Lord Jesus and the way of salvation. He had rebuffed me, telling me he had his own beliefs. At his funeral the hymn "Blessed Assurance, Jesus is mine" was sung. Why? For what reason? That man didn't believe. He had no assurance of heaven. Jesus was not "his" at all. Unless he had a change of heart and was converted in the closing moments of his life, he is now in hell and will be cast into the lake of fire with everyone else who has rejected the gospel. Why sing a hymn, as though he had gone to be with the Lord he rejected? I didn't attend his funeral, but someone who did said of the hymn: "Well, we don't know what good it might do." It would do no good at all for that man, I said. It was too late. But it is not too late for you, dear reader. Put your trust in the sinless Savior today, my friend, and your sinful soul will be counted free, as was mine.

Because the sinless Savior died,
My sinful soul is counted free;
For God the Just is satisfied
To look on Him and pardon me,
To look on Him and pardon me.

God does not judge us by weighing up our good deeds versus our bad deeds, for no amount of good deeds can save us. God's basis for judging us is our acceptance or rejection of His beloved Son. The Lord Jesus made it abundantly clear: "For God so loved the world that he gave his only begotten Son, that whosoever believeth in him should not perish, but have everlasting life. For God sent not his son into the world to condemn the world; but that the world through him might be saved. He that believeth on him (Jesus) is not condemned, but he that believeth not is condemned already, because he hath not believed in the name of the only begotten son of God." John 3:16–18

This book is copyright and may not be reproduced, but this chapter alone can be copied freely. My hope is that some of what I write may get into the hands of people who desperately need to hear the truth and be pointed in the right direction — the narrow way that leads to Heaven. For updates on what is happening in the world that points to the soon return of the Lord, check out our website daily, www.thefreepressonline.co.uk.

Chapter 3

The Church That Banned the Bible
by Alan Franklin

In March 1994 leading evangelicals and Roman Catholics signed a declaration called: "Evangelicals and Catholics together for the third millennium." This document says that Catholics and Protestants who have worked together in opposing abortion and pornography should "finally accept each other as Christians… and stop proselytizing each other's flocks." Many people in the Church of England, Lutherans, Baptists and other major denominations are now convinced that Catholics are their fellow believers in the one true God.

In Britain it has become almost impossible to point out Catholic doctrinal errors. Somewhere in Britain a mother and teenage daughter went on a Bible Society sponsored walk, organized, as far as they were aware, by the independent Baptist church which their family attended. They did not realize that the Bible Society was now an ecumenical organization, or they would not have been on the walk and certainly would not have given any money.

On the last leg of the walk a middle-aged man joined the walkers and ended up chatting to the teenage girl and a middle aged lady from the Baptist church. The pair soon realized the man was a Catholic and began witnessing to him. The lady remarked that she was glad that Catholics were now allowed to read the Bible, and the man replied that they had always been allowed to do that. This, of course, is not true. The Bible was banned by the Catholic Church for centuries; it was actually on The Index, the list of banned books.

The girl told the Catholic man that the Bible clearly teaches that Jesus' death was the one and only sacrifice for sin, while the Catholic

Church offers the "sacrifice of the mass" over and over again. At this point an elder of the (Baptist) church interrupted the conversation and put an end to any further dialogue along those lines. He said those religious differences were all long ago and things were much better now, we didn't burn each other at the stake any more and wasn't it lovely weather for a walk? Later they all learned that the man on the walk was a Catholic priest.

The teenager was upset by this incident. After years of trying to witness to girls and teachers at school, and students and lecturers at her college, and often being accused of being an intolerant bigot, she had now been firmly stopped — by a church elder for whom she had great respect. The next day at their church the girl and her mother were accused by the wife of another elder of being "subversive" for lending tapes and videos to other people at church. The tapes were mostly by Dave Hunt and Christian creationists.

They were also told they were arrogant to think they could judge who was and was not Christian. In fact it is the word of God which says who is. Someone who thinks they are saved by membership of a church, by receiving sacraments regularly, who can pay for "time off" in purgatory, who wears magic scapulars for "the grace of a happy death," who sings hymns to Mary, "co-redemptrix" with Jesus — I'm sorry, that person does not believe the gospel and has not been saved. They are religious, but they are not born-again believers in Jesus. They are Catholics, believers in the Catholic Church, a superstitious, pagan organization which masquerades as Christian. The Catholic gospel is not the true gospel; it is a false gospel, and people who believe a false gospel are not saved, they are deceived. It is our job to undeceive them.

It is tragic that Christians trying to do this are gagged by their own elders. Later the Catholic priest phoned the church to complain about the pair who had so offended him on the country walk. I wonder if he is one of the priests who have consecrated his life to Mary, as thousands of priests have, at the urging of the Pope?

The teenager gave this account of her conversation with the priest: "One of the first things to be said was that the testimony of Scripture bore witness against the Roman Catholic Church. In illustration of this point we gave the second commandment, which makes it plain that we are not to create images for ourselves of anything that is in heaven or on the earth and bow down to them. This goes contrary to Roman Catholic practice, for Catholics do bow the knee to statues and images of saints.

"After discussion on this point we moved on to the Roman Catholic teaching of transubstantiation. The Roman Catholic was stating Jesus' words: 'This is My body.' We pointed out that Jesus was standing there in His physical body as he spoke those words and that he also made metaphorical statements elsewhere, such as 'I am the door.'

"We went on to tell the man that Jesus' death on the cross was the final payment for sin, and that this fact is denied by the Roman Catholic Church, which teaches that Jesus' sacrifice is literally repeated again and again at each 'sacrifice of the mass.'

"No Roman Catholic can have unity with us if we believe that salvation comes through faith in Christ alone, and that the sacrifice of Jesus at Calvary made a full and complete atonement for our sin. Neither should we attempt to make Roman Catholics feel they have any unity with us, for the Roman Catholic Church teaches that punishment for sin falls on individuals, who can be exempted from this punishment through good works, attending mass, and even through the payment of money (indulgences). Surely this should produce within any believer a righteous indignation? It is no less than blasphemy to state that anything can secure exemption from punishment for our sin, when the shedding of our Lord's blood was supposedly insufficient to do so.

"You might argue that many Roman Catholics do not fully understand the teachings of their church, and that many have hearts which sincerely seek after God. It is our duty to tell such people the truth, not to leave them floundering in the darkness of a heretical, anti-Christ religion. Anyway, the man we were talking to clearly knew the doctrines of the church and was ardently defending them.

"People need to be freed from Roman Catholicism by the blood of Jesus, no less than they need to be freed from other false religions. Just because the errors of Roman Catholicism are more subtle than those of other religions, they are no less dangerous (indeed they are far more so). Yes, it is divisive to tell people the truth, and the cross is an offence to people. You may also think that we should not be confrontational, but which biblical figure followed a policy of 'no confrontation'? Certainly none of those who were sent to declare God's truth to people. Should we have befriended the man first? Where is it done so in the Bible?" (End of the girl's letter.)

So it was that a clear-minded young girl saw the obvious, when church leaders, including the Archbishop of Canterbury and any number of other top church leaders, seemingly cannot. What a sorry state our churches have come to in Great Britain, past home to great men of the gospel like Whitfield and Wesley, Spurgeon and Knox.

Unfortunately the Church of England, the Anglican church, is almost as bad as the church of Rome. We now have Protestant cathedrals, like Winchester in Hampshire, inviting Catholic preachers in to say the mass! This cathedral, where they now solicit admission fees as if to Disneyland, has a place in the hearts of the Franklin family because it was to this building that God led my wife, Pat, as she was on the point of conversion. While on a visit there, she was prompted by the Holy Spirit to open the Book of Common Prayer and read: "Except a man be born again he cannot enter the kingdom of God." Yet now, for the first time since the 16th century, a Roman Catholic cardinal has celebrated mass in Latin at the high altar. Michael Scott-Joynt, the Bishop of Winchester, is twinning Winchester with the Roman Catholic cathedral of Florence and invited Cardinal Piovanelli, the Archbishop of Florence, to spend the weekend at Winchester, not only officiating at mass, but giving the Sunday evensong service.

Cathedral spokesman Simon Barwood told the press: "It's a real symbol of the sisterhood between Anglicans and Roman Catholics. Bishop Michael has just been to Florence visiting the cathedral for a week and the millennium celebration of our patron saint, St. Swithun, seemed the perfect occasion to return the hospitality and sign the twinning agreement. We have several different partners attached to the cathedral now. It's symbolic, but also practical. There are exchange opportunities and a new atmosphere of tolerance and understanding." How nice for them. What next, links with the Hindus and Moslems, in a spirit of tolerance and understanding? The pope has already done this, of course, even including tree worshippers in a giant ecumenical service. Only true Christians weren't invited. These "church leaders" wallow in their ignorance and flaunt it.

This criticism applies particularly to many so-called Christian bookshops, which are so stuffed full of crucifixes and rosaries that they don't seem to have room on their shelves for Foxe's Book of Martyrs, which tells the true story of horrific persecution of Christians down through the ages. When I tried to get certain of these bookshops in my home area to stock my first video and later my book *EU: Final World Empire* I was told that it was too divisive and might upset the Catholics, who were good customers. When I delivered a lecture on the Catholic creed to one shop manager who had rosaries on his shelves, he became agitated and told me to keep my voice down or Catholics would hear. I said this was my intention! We must always remember to love Roman Catholics, for most of them are in ignorance of what their church teaches and has done through the ages. Is it love to keep them in ignorance?

I worked for years with some pleasant Roman Catholic people, but it is not loving to allow them to proceed merrily to hell, believing that the sacraments, the Virgin Mary etc will save them, plus the occasional fumble with the rosary beads. I have often noticed how fearful and superstitious they are: for example, most would not pass me on the stairs of our offices as "it brings bad luck." What we must bring to such folk — our divine commission — is the truth about Jesus, the only conduit between man and God. It seems the need for compromise and unity, together with a certain profit motive, is stopping the clear truth of the Bible reaching denominational and nominal Christians, particularly those under Catholic deception. We should be more interested in prophets than profits!

My wife and I have been accused — often in hostile terms — of being too critical and "unloving," for daring to confront some unbiblical comment or policy. Yet God calls us to be discerning and to speak out against heresy: Paul did it all the time and Jude instructs us to contend for the faith. This is not what most churchgoers in Great Britain want to hear today. The people have itching ears for false doctrine, have no love for the truth and do not want to hear any different. Their ignorance, even in once godly denominations, would seem to make them very happy.

We often meet truly discerning, well read and wise older Christians who tell us they "cannot find a church." The same thing is happening across the USA. I am privileged to speak at the East Coast Prophecy Conferences in Pennsylvania put on by Southwest Radio Church of Oklahoma City. One after another delegates to the conferences have told us they had to leave their churches. One family had to leave the church their grandfather founded. They all felt they had no choice but to leave because of false doctrines which were now taught. Time and again we met people in this situation; people lamenting the friends they had left behind, but people who knew they could not stay in an organization where apostasy was taught from the pulpit. This is clearly the Laodicean church age. Interestingly enough, we have found that just about the only born again people there and also in Britain who are still content with their churches are those in the Brethren, or some evangelicals and Baptists who stick like glue to the scriptures.

Not only does the Christian church not know the history of Protestantism, it doesn't know biblical history, which is even more serious. Our daughter Annie and her friend spent three weeks at the wonderful summer Bible camp held in New York state by Dr. Arnold Fruchtenbaum, learning about the Bible from a Jewish perspective (Arnold is a Messianic Jew, saved as a teenager). On returning to her home church, an Anglican (Episcopalian) center, Annie's friend was asked, in all seriousness: "What is the point of learning about the Bible from a Jewish point of view?"

An anti-semitic stance is behind some churches' attitudes: when my wife grew up in the Roman Catholic faith in the mid-west there was an underlying anti-semitism. Among the Catholics she grew up amongst, the word 'Jews' was seldom used without the prefix "damn." This is just one sign that Catholicism is incompatible with biblical Christianity. We are not to seek unity with a false religious system with its roots in pagan Babylon.

In recent times Catholic commentators and apologists have glossed over the disgraceful complicity of the Vatican in Hitler's holocaust of the Jews. However, God made sure the truth came out. In a Roman flea market, of all places, a journalist antiquarian book collector called Fabrizio Coisson found documents that prove that Pope Pius XII knew all about Nazi atrocities. This Pope, of whom it has often been said that he turned a blind eye to Hitler, who was a Catholic, was given a daily account of the atrocities of Hitler's henchmen. Francis D'Arcy Godolphin Osborne was the British minister to the Holy See and typed out a daily report for the Pope. He culled this from British broadcasts, picked up in the Vatican where he took refuge in 1940. Mr. Coisson said he was astonished to find a signed note in which the British diplomat describes how, on a daily basis, he typed out the BBC broadcasts and gave them to the Pope. Osborne died in Rome in 1964 and it is thought that some of his possessions were sold and eventually found their way on to the market stall.

The Times, published in London, carried a story on May 24, 2000 headed: "British envoy sent Pope bulletins on the Holocaust." The story quoted Professor Owen Chadwick of Cambridge University, author of "Britain and The Vatican During The Second World War", as saying the find was "remarkable," while Jesuit historian Father Pierre Blet admitted it was astonishing. The reports in the market documents give a detailed account of Jewish deportations, mass killings and "inhuman experiments" and may at least slow plans to beatify Pius XII. Rabbi Martin Hier, of the Simon Wiesenthal Centre in Los Angeles, was quoted in *The Times* as saying that it would desecrate the memory of the Holocaust victims to beatify a man "who sat in silence on the throne of St. Peter and watched the trains take Jews across Europe to the death camps."

Francis Osborne had arrived in Rome in 1936, to represent Britain at The Vatican. He was an admirer of Pope Pius. However, he closely followed Allied broadcasts and began putting together compilations of what he called "British wireless news" for the Pope. He emphasized the suffering of civilians in occupied Europe and German — "crimes against humanity." In October of 1940 he told the Pope that the Germans were actively promoting anti-Semitism in Hungary, Romania and Bulgaria. In 1941 his tone had become more dramatic, as the Nazis "committed atrocities in the name of the myth of the superior race." He also put it in writing for the Pope that the Germans were "conducting experiments on sick and mentally deficient children in Germany," and noted that Hitler had vowed to "liquidate the Jews for at least 1000 years." The Pope was also told that Polish Jews were being murdered and deported en masse and that: "In Poland they have announced that Jews may in future only travel by railway after obtaining a special permit, and then only by slow train."

In 1943 Osborne's campaign was intensified and he told the Pope that in Slovakia : "77 per cent of the Jewish population has been deported to an unknown destination, which probably signifies death... and the number of Jews in the Warsaw Ghetto has been reduced by 400,000 since last July — there are barely 35,000 left."

The writer John Cornwell had earlier claimed in his book *"Hitler's Pope"* that Pius not only failed to speak out against Nazi persecution as Pope, but that earlier, as Papal ambassador (Nuncio) in Berlin in the 1920s and Secretary of State in the 1930s, he helped put Hitler into power by suppressing German Catholic resistance to the Nazis. It is clear that there was no love for the Jews at the very top of the Roman Catholic Church, yet the whole concept of the Messiah is a Jewish one. It was the Jews who were looking for a Messiah, the Jews who had been told they were God's chosen people, the Jews to whom God sent the prophets, the Jews who were saved time and again from their enemies, the Jews to whom God sent great leaders, the Jews to whom God spoke directly, the Jews who provided the disciples — and Jesus was a Jew. It was the Hebrew scriptures which contained the Messianic prophecies and if Jesus is not the Messiah of the Jews, he can't be our Messiah either. Suddenly you have no basis for Christianity.

Years ago I recall the leader of a black church pointing out: "Jesus wasn't white." He certainly wasn't the blue-eyed, flaxen haired savior depicted in many stained glass windows. He almost certainly had olive-colored skin and dark hair, as you would expect from someone born in the Mediterranean area, which makes it all the more amazing that there are churches in America and elsewhere dedicated to racism, yet calling themselves "Christian". Yes, Jesus was a Jew, a fact people sometimes need reminding of, but he came for every inhabitant of the world. All the more surprising then that, in these last days, you can be called "racist" for telling people that Jesus is the only way to Heaven. This happened to our daughter, as she tried to witness to a fellow student. It happened to a teacher friend of mine who was told that he couldn't teach "Christian exclusiveness" in religious studies. After all, all roads lead to God, don't they?

There is a difference between real Christianity and Catholicism, a difference the evil rulers of the world recognize far more than the gullible Christians of western Protestantism. Some years ago some Americans I know ventured down to Mexico to help build an evangelical church. The local believers had tried to build it, but had been shot at by the Roman Catholics of the area. They said to the work team from the USA: "They won't dare shoot at you." So the church was built, one of the builders being a brother-in-law of mine. If you want to see the difference between Christianity and Catholicism, go to South America. There's not a lot of ecumenism about...

It is a matter of historical record that the Catholic Church has tried to keep the Bible out of the hands of ordinary people. The Catholic Bible was in Latin, which few people could read, and they wanted to keep it that way. Just a few dates:

- 1229 A.D. Council of Toulouse, Canon 14: "We prohibit also that the laity (the ordinary people) should be permitted to have the books of the Old or New Testament..."
- 1559 Index Librorum Prohibitorum — Pope Pius IV starts an Index of Forbidden Books condemning the works of "arch-heretics" Luther and Calvin, including translations of the New Testament. You needed permission in writing to read a Catholic translation of the Bible, and if you had a Bible in the common language without written permission, your sins could not be forgiven unless you turned in the Bible.
- Sept 8, 1713 Encyclical Unigenitus from Pope Clement XI — condemning the "error" of stating that every person should study Scripture.
- May 5, 1824 Encyclical Ubi Primum from Pope Leo XII — condemning Bibles printed in the vernacular (the spoken language of the people) as a "wretched undertaking".

- May 8, 1844 Encyclical Inter Praecipuas (On Biblical Societies) — Pope Gregory XVI condemns "secret gatherings" for
  the reading of scripture. "We again condemn ... biblical societies ..."
- 1897 Pope Leo XIII *Apostolic Constitution Officiorum ac
  Munerum* — "All versions of the Holy Bible, in any vernacular
  language, made by non-Catholics are prohibited; and especially
  those published by the Bible societies, which have been more
  that once condemned by the Roman Pontiffs (Popes)..."
- 1930 Forward to the *Index of Prohibited Books:* "Those who
  would put the Scriptures indiscriminately into the hands of the
  people ... (these) counterfeit champions of the inspired book
  hold the Bible to be the sole source of Divine Revelation and
  cover with abuse and trite sarcasm the Catholic and Roman
  Church."
- 1983 Code of Canon Law (the current Catholic law on Bibles
  in the common language) — Translations of the Bible cannot
  be published unless approved by the Apostolic See (the Papacy
  in Rome) "annotated with necessary and sufficient explanations."

And those are some of the reasons we say again that the Roman
Catholic Church is: the church that banned the Bible. We are sorry to
say that the suppression of Scripture did not stop there. Incredibly, the
Protestant Reformation did not go nearly far enough — and after the
break with Rome, even the Church of England banned the English Bible! Courageous preachers called Lollards were burned at the stake
with their English Bibles hung round their necks. John Bunyan, beloved
author of *Pilgrim's Progress*, fell foul of the Church of England and was
made to serve 14 years in Bedford Jail near Cambridge for preaching
the gospel.

In the year 2000 as part of the celebrations in England at the turn of
the millennium, excerpts from *Pilgrim's Progress* were read out in one
of the great London cathedrals by some actress. We were sickened. At
no time did anyone say, "We're standing in one of the great Church of
England cathedrals, the religious organization which burned people to
death for possessing an English Bible and which imprisoned great authors and preachers like John Bunyan." No, they did not say that. They
too, the Church of England, are tarred with the same wretched brush:
the church that **also** banned the Bible.

Chapter 4

Table of Truth:
the Roman Catholic Church vs. the Bible

What the Catholic Church says: **What the Bible says:**

Calvary	Calvary
Jesus is offered **again and again** as a sacrifice at every mass.	There was only **one** sacrifice, at Calvary, and that was sufficient for all time. '…we are sanctified through the offering of the body of Jesus Christ **once** for all.' '…**one** sacrifice for sins forever…' 'For by **one offering** he hath perfected forever them that are sanctified.' '…there is **no more offering** for sin.' All these scriptures are from Hebrews Chapter 10 '…who needeth not daily to offer up sacrifice… for this He did **once**…' Hebrews 7:27
Salvation (being saved from hell)	**Salvation (being saved from hell)**
You **might** get to heaven if you are a good Catholic.	You will **definitely** get to heaven if you trust in the Lord Jesus. 'Verily, verily, I say unto you: he that **believeth** on me **hath** (al-

What the Catholic Church says:	What the Bible says:
	ready has) everlasting life.' (This means you just have to believe; your salvation does not depend on any denomination). John 6:47 'He that **believeth** on the Son hath everlasting life...' John 3:36 '(Peter speaking) And it shall come to pass, that **whosoever** shall call on the name of the Lord shall be saved.' Acts 2:21
Faith	**Faith**
The Council of Trent excommunicates and condemns to hell anyone who says that we are made right (justified) with God by faith, trusting in Christ's sacrifice at Calvary. 'Let him be anathema (condemned).' This 'infallible' Roman Catholic statement from the 16th century still stands and can never be revoked. The purpose of the Council of Trent was to condemn Protestant teaching of scripture.	'For by grace are ye saved through faith; and that not of yourselves: it is the gift of God.' Ephesians 2:8 If you believe this scripture, the Roman Catholic Church would condemn you to hell for eternity.
Who can condemn you to hell?	**Who can condemn you to hell?**
The Pope thinks he can condemn you for many reasons, but he is just a mere man. No man has the power to send anyone to hell. The Catholic church claims for itself the power that belongs to Christ alone.	Only the Lord Jesus Christ can condemn someone to hell. Only He has the keys of hell and of death. He is the righteous judge, not any man, not any religious institution. 'I... have the keys of hell and of death.' Rev 1:18. See also Rev 19:11 and 20:11–15.
Who gets to heaven?	**Who gets to heaven?**
In the Catholic schools I attended we were always led to believe the Catholic Church was the one true	'He that believeth on Me hath everlasting life.' John 6:47 'For God so loved the world that

What the Catholic Church says:	What the Bible says:
church and only Catholics would get to heaven. Pope Benedict XVI issued a document in 2007 stating that Christ "established here on earth" only one Church "…This Church, constituted and organised in this world as a society, subsists in the Catholic Church…"	He gave His only begotten Son, that whosoever believeth in Him should not perish, but have everlasting life.' John 3:16 'Believe on the Lord Jesus Christ, and thou shalt be saved, and thy house.' (Paul speaking to the prison keeper.) Acts 16:31 'For you are all the children of God by faith in Christ Jesus.' Galatians 3:26 Whoever has saving faith in Christ will be with Him in heaven, regardless of denominational membership.
How do you become a Christian?	**How do you become a Christian?**
By being baptized (usually as a baby). Then you have to keep doing what the Roman Catholic Church tells you — going to mass, receiving the 'sacraments', etc. If you don't keep doing all this, you lose your salvation.	The Lord Jesus tells us in the gospel of John Chap 3 verse 3 that we have to be 'born again' — born spiritually. Our spirit inside us has to be born, like our physical body was born. This happens when we place our faith in Jesus Christ, trusting in His blood sacrifice to atone (pay the penalty) for all our sins. Until this spiritual rebirth happens, the Bible tells us we are 'dead in trespasses and sins.' (Ephesians 2:1; Colossians 2:13). Once this spiritual birth takes place, we are 'sealed' with the Holy Spirit (Ephesians 1:13 and 4:30). The Holy Spirit takes up residence in our spirit and will never leave us. His presence in us is a guarantee of our full salvation. You can go to church every day of your life and still not be born again.

What the Catholic Church says:	What the Bible says:
Communion	**Communion**
Jesus is "mystically" present in the wafer and the wine. When the priest says the words, the bread and wine change into the actual body and blood of Jesus Christ, while keeping the appearance of bread and wine	The communion service is symbolic, and the purpose is to help us remember Jesus' great sacrifice for us. 'And he took bread, and gave thanks, and brake it, and gave unto them, saying, This is my body which is given for you: this do **in remembrance** of me.' Luke 22:19 '…Take, eat: this is my body, which is broken for you: this do **in remembrance** of me.' 1 Corinthians 11:24 '…as oft as ye drink it, **in remembrance** of me.' 1 Corinthians 11:25 The Lord's Supper (the bread and wine) is simply to help us remember that He shed His blood for us and died for our sins. There is no magic change in the bread or the wine. The bread is still bread and the wine is still wine. No special person called a 'priest' is needed to say anything over the bread and wine.
Priests	**Priests**
Catholic priests are special people who stand between God and ordinary believers. Only a Catholic priest can say the special formula which changes the bread and wine into the body and blood of the Lord Jesus.	All believers are members of 'a royal priesthood, a holy nation, a peculiar people… which in time past were not a people, but are now the people of God…' 1 Peter 2:9, 10 The Lord Jesus is our high priest who has gone before us into the heavenlies.

What the Catholic Church says:	What the Bible says:
	When believers are together they can at any time break bread and share wine together in remembrance of our Lord's great sacrifice for us.
Prayer	**Prayer**
It is good to pray the rosary (53 Hail Marys and 6 Our Fathers).	'But when ye pray, use not vain repetitions, as the heathen do, for they think that they shall be heard for their much speaking.' Matthew 6:7
Our Mediator (the one who goes between us and God)	**Our Mediator (the one who goes between us and God)**
Mary is co-mediator between us and God.	'For there is one God, and **one mediator** between God and men, the man Christ Jesus…' 1 Timothy 2:5
Mary	**Mary**
Mary was conceived without sin.	'**All** have sinned and come short of the glory of God." Romans 3:23 '(Mary speaking) And my spirit hath rejoiced in God **my Savior**.' Luke 1:47 Mary too needed a Savior. She too needed forgiveness for sin.
Mary is the 'Queen of Heaven'.	The 'Queen of Heaven' is a pagan goddess. God was ashamed of the Israelites for worshipping this demonic being. See Jeremiah 7:18–20
Mary will intercede for you.	For there is one God, and **one mediator** also between God and men, the man Christ Jesus… 1 Timothy 2:5
'Blessed is the womb that bore You (Jesus).'	'On the contrary, blessed are those who hear the word of

What the Catholic Church says:	What the Bible says:
Mary is the mother of God.	God and observe it.' Luke 11:28 The Lord Jesus replying to a woman in the crowd. 'My mother and My brethren are these who hear the word of God and do it.' Luke 8:21
Scripture (the Bible)	**Scripture (the Bible)**
The canons and decrees of the Roman church are more important than the scriptures in the Bible.	The Bible, the Word of God, is absolutely foremost. 'All scripture is given by inspiration of God...' 2 Timothy 3:16 'Heaven and earth shall pass away, but my words shall not pass away.' Matthew 24:35, and Mark 13:31, and Luke 21:33. 'Forever, O Lord, thy word is settled in heaven.' Psalm 119:89 '...if any man shall add unto these things (scripture), God shall add unto him the plagues that are written in this book...' Revelation 22:18 The Catholic Church has added many things.
"Father"	**"Father"**
The Pope is the 'Holy Father' and every priest must be called 'Father'.	'Call no man your father upon the earth: for one is your Father, which is in heaven.' Matthew 23:9
The Pope	**The Pope**
The Pope is leader of the church on earth.	'...ye are all brethren (brothers).' (No big chief.) Matthew 23:8 'Woe unto you, scribes and Pharisees, hypocrites! For ye are like unto whited sepulchers, which indeed appear beautiful outward, but are within full of dead men's bones, and of all uncleanness.' Matthew 23:27

What the Catholic Church says:	What the Bible says:
Peter was the first pope.	'The elders who are among you I (Peter) exhort, who am also **an elder**...' 1 Peter 5:1 'But when Cephas (Peter) came to Antioch, I (Paul) opposed him to his face, because he stood condemned.' Galatians 2:11 At the first ever church council in Jerusalem, James concluded the council's deliberations by saying, 'Therefore it is my judgment...' and his judgment stood. He and not Peter made the crucial pronouncement. Acts 15:19 Peter was not the pope, because there was no such office. He was an apostle, because he had been with Christ and he was an eyewitness of the resurrection, as were all the apostles. No one after that generation is an eyewitness of the resurrection.
The popes are all in a direct line of descent from Peter.	Please do a bit of research and uncover for yourself the disgraceful chain of perverts, murderers and thieves who have 'sat in Peter's chair' and worn the 'shoes of the fisherman'. Learn how many of the popes distinguished themselves by ordering the papal army to hunt down and murder true Christians like the Waldenses and Albegenses in Europe. It is thought that millions of true believers in Jesus died martyrs' deaths by order of the Popes of

What the Catholic Church says:	**What the Bible says:**
	Rome. Please read Foxe's Book of Martyrs. America was partly settled by Huguenots and others fleeing from the murderous agents of the popes.
Purgatory	**Purgatory**
When you die, you go to purgatory to burn for your sins. Jesus' sacrifice was not enough. You have to pay for your own sins.	'Verily I say unto thee; **today** shalt thou be with me in paradise.' Luke 23:43 '...willing rather to be absent from the body, and to be present with the Lord.' 2 Corinthians 5:8 'having a desire to depart and to be with Christ...' Phillipians 1:23 'Truly I say to you, **all sins** shall be forgiven the sons of men... 'Mark 3:28 Burning in purgatory was a concept that started in ancient Babylon, when the pagan priests were paid to get the dead person out of the flames. The Roman church latched on to this concept to extort money from grieving families. The Lord Jesus paid **all** the penalty for sin at Calvary. There is nothing we can add to His sacrifice.
Idols (statues)	**Idols (statues)**
Statues help us to honor the dead person.	The Second Commandment: 'Thou shalt not make unto thee any graven image, or any likeness of anything that is in heaven

What the Catholic Church says:	What the Bible says:
	above, or that is in the earth beneath... Thou shalt not bow down (kneel) thyself to them...' Exodus 20:4–5 'And they served their idols: which were a snare unto them.' Psalm 106:36 'Their land also is full of idols; they worship the work of their own hands, that which their own fingers have made: and the mean man boweth down and the great man humbleth himself: therefore forgive them not.' Isaiah 2:8 'Neither be ye idolaters...' 1 Corinthians 10:7 '...flee from idolatry.' 1Corinthians 10:14 An idol is anything or any being you worship or 'idolize' or address prayers to other than God Himself. God alone is to be worshipped. He alone is the object of our prayers and adoration. Not dead saints. Not Mary.
Saints	**Saints**
"Saints" are very holy, dead people.	Saints are living believers. If you are a born again believer in Jesus, you are a saint. '...receive her in the Lord, as becometh saints...' Romans 16:2 'Paul... unto the church of God which is at Corinth, with all the saints (living believers) which are in all Achaia...' 2 Corinthians 1:1

What the Catholic Church says:	What the Bible says:
	'Paul... to the saints which are at Ephesus...' Ephesians 1:1 '...to all the saints... at Phillippi' Philippians 1:1 '...to the saints... at Colosse...' Colossians 1:2
The Rock	**The Rock**
The church was founded upon the rock — Peter.	Jesus Christ is the Rock of our salvation. '...Jesus Christ...this is the stone... which is become the head of the corner.' Acts 4:10–11 'I lay in Zion a chief cornerstone (Jesus), elect, precious, and he that believeth on him shall not be confounded.' 1 Peter 2:6–8 '... that Rock was Christ.' 1 Corinthians 10:4
Celibacy	**Celibacy**
Priests and nuns should be celibate and take vows that bind them to remain celibate all their lives.	Peter was married (as were some of the other apostles). 'And when Jesus was come into Peter's house, he saw his wife's mother (Peter's mother-in-law) laid and sick of a fever.' Matthew 8:14–15 '(Paul speaking) ...let every man have his own wife, and let every woman have her own husband.' 1Corinthians 7:2 'A bishop then must be blameless, the husband of one wife...' 1 Timothy 3:2 'Now the Spirit speaketh expressly that in the latter times some shall depart from the faith, giving

What the Catholic Church says:	What the Bible says:
	heed to seducing spirits and **doctrines of devils**... forbidding to marry...' 1 Timothy 4:1–3 Forbidding people to marry is a doctrine of devils. The Roman church began this practice to stop married priests leaving all their property to their children. The Vatican wanted their land, homes and money. I am told that the tombs of married priests and their families can still be seen in Rome.
Church services	**Church services**
Church services should be highly structured with only certain people allowed to officiate, saying only certain things that are prescribed in advance.	'...when ye come together, every one of you (men) hath a psalm, hath a doctrine, hath a tongue, hath a revelation, hath an interpretation. Let all things be done unto edifying.' 1 Corinthians 14:26
Charities	**Charities**
You will be expected as a Catholic to give to the charities connected with the church.	Check this out! We were surprised to find that one of these had Catholic executives earning six figures. Very charitable to them! Plus a pension no doubt. Plus whatever else, possibly a car, expenses, medical etc. So the next time they ask for your money, ask them a few questions, like: Does the charity have paid executives? How much do they earn? Pension? Etc.

Written by Pat Franklin, a 'cradle Catholic' educated at Roman Catholic schools in America. I read the New Testament for myself (a Catholic version of the Bible) in England in 1981 and saw that Roman Catholicism was not right, but that salvation was by faith in Christ alone. I knelt down in my bedroom and confessed my sins to the Lord Jesus and begged Him to let me be one of His people. From that day I have belonged to Him.

Chapter 5

Table of Truth:
Islam vs. the Bible

Founder: Mohammed, camel driver of desert caravans in the 7th century A.D. in present day Saudi Arabia. Mohammed could not read or write.

Visions: He began seeing visions of a supernatural being while meditating in a cave. At first he was terrified and thought it was a "jinn", an evil spirit. His wife convinced him the being was from God. The being claimed to be the angel Gabriel.

Spread: Within decades Mohammed's followers had conquered the Middle East and North Africa. The goal is to conquer the world for Allah.

Headquarters: Mecca, Saudi Arabia. There are now mosques and Islamic centers throughout Europe and America.

Numbers: Said to be 1.2 billion, or 22 per cent of the world's population.

Islam says:	The Bible says:
Jesus Christ	**Jesus Christ**
Jesus is not God.	The Lord Jesus Christ is God. "In the beginning was the Word (Jesus, often referred to as the Word of God), and the Word was with God, and the Word was God." John 1:1 "And Thomas answered and said unto him, My Lord and my God." John 20:28

Islam says:	The Bible says:
	"…let all the angels of God worship him (Jesus)." Hebrews 1:6 "And they worshipped him (Jesus)…" Luke 24:52 Only God is ever to be worshipped, according to the First Commandment. Jesus is definitely God, the Second Person of the Trinity.
The Son of God	**The Son of God**
God has no son. "God is only one god; he is far above having a son…" Sura 4:171	"Thou art **my beloved Son**; in thee I am well pleased." Luke 3:22 (at the baptism of the Lord Jesus). "For God so loved the world that He gave **His only begotten Son**, that whosoever believeth in him should not perish, but have everlasting life." John 3:16
The Messiah (Savior) of Israel	**The Messiah (Savior) of Israel**
"Those who say, "God is the Messiah, the son of Mary," are defying the truth." Sura 5:17	"He (Andrew) found his own brother Simon, and said unto him, We have found the Messiah, which is… the Christ." John 1:41
The cross	**The cross**
Jesus was not crucified, and did not die. "They did not kill him, nor did they crucify him…" Sura 4:157	Jesus WAS crucified. "And they crucified him…" Matthew 27:35 "And when they had crucified him…" Mark 15:24 "And when they came to the place, which is called Calvary, there they crucified him..." Luke 23:33 "(Golgotha) where they crucified him…" John 19:18
The death of the Lord Jesus	**The death of the Lord Jesus**
Jesus did not die.	"And Jesus cried with a loud

Islam says:	The Bible says:
	voice, and gave up the ghost." Mark 15:37 "Jesus, when he had cried again with a loud voice, yielded up the ghost." Matthew 27:50 "Father, into thy hands I commend my spirit: and having said thus, he gave up the ghost." Luke 23:46 "But when they came to Jesus, and saw that he was dead already, they brake not his legs." John 19:33 All four gospels testify to the death on the cross of the Lord Jesus as a substitute for us, paying the penalty for the sins of all who trust in Him.
Burial	**Burial**
Jesus did not die, therefore He was never buried, but was taken up.	"This man (Joseph of Arimathaea) went unto Pilate, and begged the body of Jesus. And he took it down, and wrapped it in linen, and laid it in a sepulcher that was hewn in stone, wherein never man before was laid." Luke 23:52, 53
The resurrection	**The resurrection**
No death, so no resurrection.	"...I know that ye seek Jesus, which was crucified. He is not here: for **He is risen**, as He said." (words of the angel who rolled back the stone so that Jesus' friends could see into the empty tomb.) Matthew 28:5–6 "Ye seek Jesus of Nazareth which was crucified: He is risen: He is not here: behold the place where they laid Him." (words of the an-

Islam says:	The Bible says:
	gel) Mark 16:6 "…Why seek ye the living among the dead? He is not here, but is **risen**…" Luke 24:5–6 "Thomas, because thou hast seen Me, thou hast believed: blessed are they that have not seen, and yet have believed." John 20:29
Virgin birth	**Virgin birth**
"In god's eyes Jesus is just like Adam: He created him from dust, said to him, 'Be', and he was.' Sura 3:59	"Behold, a virgin shall be with child, and shall bring forth a son, and they shall call his name Emmanuel, which being interpreted is, God with us." Matthew 1:23
Getting to Heaven	**Getting to Heaven**
Even Mohammed was not sure he would get to Heaven. He taught that the righteous would get to Heaven if their good deeds outweighed their bad deeds. At the end of his life Mohammed said: 'By Allah, though I am the apostle of Allah, yet I do not know what Allah will do to me.' Vol. 5:266, Hadith	"He that believeth on the Son hath everlasting life…" John 3:36 "…He that believeth on Me hath everlasting life." John 6:47
Forgiveness of sins	**Forgiveness of sins**
No assurance unless you die fighting. 'Let those of you who are willing to trade the life of this world for the life to come, fight in god's way. To anyone who fights in god's way, whether killed or victorious, we shall give a great reward.' Sura 4:74. Suicide bombers believe that because of their murderous act, their sins will be	"Christ died for our sins…" 1 Corinthians 15:3 "If we confess our sins, He is faithful and just to forgive us our sins and to cleanse us from all unrighteousness." 1 John 1:9 "Jesus Christ the righteous: He is the propitiation for our sins and not for ours only, but also for the sins of the whole world.'

Islam says:	The Bible says:
forgiven and that they — and a whole troop of their relatives — will go straight to Paradise.	1 John 2:1'2 "…while we were yet sinners, Christ died for us." Romans 5:8 "…being now justified by His blood, we shall be saved from wrath through Him." Romans 5:9
The way to God	**The way to God**
Good works, but no one is ever sure.	"I am the way, the truth and the life: no man cometh unto the Father, but by me." John 14:6
Salvation	**Salvation**
"Every soul is held in pledge for its deeds." Sura 74:38	"…him that cometh to me I will in no wise cast out." John 6:37
Other faiths	**Other faiths**
"We will strike panic into the disbelievers' hearts because they attribute partners to God…" Sura 3:151 "Fight those of the People of the Book (Jews and Christians) who do not truly believe in god and the last day, who do not forbid what god and his messenger (Mohammed) have forbidden… until they pay the tax and agree to submit." Sura 9:29	"Stand fast therefore in the liberty wherewith Christ hath made us free, and be not entangled again with the yoke of bondage." Galatians 5:1
Those who leave the faith	**Those who leave the faith**
"Whoever changes his religion, kill him." Hadith 9:57	"So then because thou art lukewarm, and neither cold nor hot, I will spue thee out of my mouth." Rev 3:16. The Lord will deal with people when He returns.
Enemies	**Enemies**
"If you do not go out and fight, god will punish you severely…" Sura 9:39	"Love your enemies, bless them that curse you, do good to them that hate you, and pray for them

Islam says:	The Bible says:
"You who believe, fight the disbelievers near you…" Sura 9:123 "Fight in god's cause against those who fight you, …Kill them wherever you encounter them and drive them out from where they drove you out, for persecution is more serious than killing…Fight them until there is no more persecution and worship is devoted to god (Allah)." Sura 2:190–193 Those who will not fight: "…we expect god to inflict punishment on you, either from himself or at our hands…" Sura 9:52 and "they are cowardly" Sura 9:56 "He who fights so that Allah's word (Islam) should be superior, then he fights in Allah's cause." Hadith, Vol. 1, Book 3, Number 125	which despitefully use you and persecute you." Words of the Lord Jesus, Matthew 5:44 "My kingdom is not of this world." John 19:36 "If someone strikes you on one cheek, turn to him the other also." Luke 6:29
Marriage in Heaven?	**Marriage in Heaven?**
Muslim men who make it to Heaven will get many wives.	There is no marriage in Heaven. "For in the resurrection they neither marry, nor are given in marriage, but are as the angels of God in heaven." Matthew 22:30 "For when they rise from the dead, they neither marry nor are given in marriage, but are as the angels which are in heaven." Mark 12:25
Heaven	**Heaven**
It is like a garden with many streams and many wives. "There will be maidens restraining their glances, untouched beforehand by man or jinn (demon	"And I saw a new heaven and a new earth: for the first heaven and the first earth were passed away; and there was no more sea." Book of Revelation, Chapter 21 —

Islam says:	The Bible says:
spirits)." Sura 55:56 "There are good-natured, beautiful maidens." Sura 55:70 "They will all sit on green cushions and fine carpets." Sura 55:76 "We pair them with beautiful-eyed maidens." Sura 52:20	the entire chapter describes the matchless, unimaginable glory to come.
Treatment of women	**Treatment of women**
"If you fear high-handedness from your wives... when you go to bed, then hit them." Sura 4:34 Female genital mutilation (female circumcision) is being carried out in the name of Allah in some places. The former Dutch Member of Parliament, Somali-born Ayaan Hirsi Ali, has described how it was done to her at the age of five. (*Jerusalem Post*, May 7, 2007) Kadra in Norway was beaten after exposing the support of Norwegian imams for the horrific practice. (*Aftenposten* April 13, 2007.)	"So ought men to love their wives as their own bodies. He that loveth his wife loveth himself." Ephesians 5:28 "...let every one of you in particular so love his wife even as himself..." Ephesians 5:33 "Husbands, love your wives..." Colossians 3:19 "Let the husband render unto the wife due benevolence." 1 Corinthians 7:3 "...the husband hath not power of his own body, but the wife." 1 Corinthians 7:4
How many wives?	**How many wives?**
"...you may marry whichever women seem good to you, two, three, or four." Sura 4:3 Mohammed, on the other hand, could have a limitless number of wives, but "this was only for you, and not the rest of the believers." Sura 33:50 Men could have slave girls in addition to wives. Mohammed had nine wives. The	"A bishop must be...the husband of one wife..." 1 Timothy 3:2 "Let the deacons be the husbands of one wife..." 1 Timothy 3:12 The Lord Jesus had no wife.

Islam says:	The Bible says:
youngest was Aisha, married to him when she was 6 or 7 and the marriage consummated when she was aged 9. (from al-Tabari Hadith, Vol. 9, p. 130, 131.) Another wife was Safiya, a captive whom Mohammed married after slaughtering her father, brother, husband and others at Khaibar. (Hadith Bukhari Vol. 2, Book 14, ch. 5, no. 68, p. 35, also Vol. 4.) Another wife was Zainab Jahsh, who was married to Mohammed's adopted son. Mohammed began to desire her after seeing her naked, and then commanded his son to divorce her so he could marry her. This was not considered wrong, because, after all, he was the prophet…	
Thieves	**Thieves**
"Cut off the hands of thieves, whether they are man or woman…" Sura 5:38. In Morocco, while on vacation, we saw a distraught young woman who ran up to us crying and holding out the stumps of her wrists. Both her hands had been chopped off.	"He who has been stealing must steal no longer, but must work, doing something useful **with his own hands**…" Ephesians 4:28
New revelation	**New revelation**
Mohammed claimed to be the last prophet.	"…many false prophets shall rise and deceive many." The Lord Jesus speaking in Matthew 24:11 The test of a false prophet is that their teaching about Jesus Christ is wrong. 1 John 4:2–3

Islam says:	The Bible says:
	You will know false prophets by their fruit. Matthew 7:15–20. Is the fruit of Islam good?
Angels	**Angels**
The angel Gabriel is said to have given Mohammed the information recorded in the Koran. "The Koran is nothing less than a revelation that is sent to him (Mohammed). It was taught to him by (an angel) with mighty powers and great strength…" Sura 53:4–5	Paul wrote: "Though we, or an angel from heaven, preach any other gospel unto you than that which we have preached unto you, let him be accursed (eternally condemned)." Galatians 1:8 "Test the spirits." 1 John 4:1 "Satan himself is transformed (masquerades) into an angel of light." 2 Corinthians 11:14
Creation of mankind	**Creation of mankind**
"He Himself created the two sexes, male and female, from an ejected drop of sperm…" Sura 53:45 (This is blasphemous theology which the ancient Egyptian pagan religion also taught.)	"And the LORD God formed man of the dust of the ground, and breathed into his nostrils the breath of life; and man became a living soul." Genesis 2:7
Swearing	**Swearing**
"I swear by the position of the stars…" Sura 56:75	"But I say unto you, swear not at all, neither by heaven, for it is God's throne, nor by the earth, for it is his footstool…" Matthew 5:34, 35
Penalty for not believing	**Penalty for not believing**
"We shall brand him on the snout!" Sura 68:16	No penalty in this world, but "…he that believeth not is condemned already, because he hath not believed in the name of the only begotten Son of God." John 3:18

Islam says:	The Bible says:
Prayer	**Prayer**
The Prophet said, "Then Allah enjoined fifty prayers on my followers…" (This was later reduced to five daily prayers.) Vol. 1, Book 8, Number 345	"But when ye pray, use not vain repetitions, as the heathen do: for they think that they shall be heard for their much speaking." The Lord Jesus speaking in Matthew 6:7
Allah's apostle said, "If one says one-hundred times in one day: 'None has the right to be worshipped but Allah, the alone who has no partners, to him belongs dominion and to him belong all the praises, and he has power over all things (i.e. omnipotent),' one will get the reward of manumitting ten slaves, and one hundred good deeds will be written in his account, and one hundred bad deeds will be wiped off or erased from his account, and on that day he will be protected from the morning till evening from Satan, and nobody will be superior to him except one who has done more than that which he has done." Hadith, Vol. 4, Book 54, Number 514	
"Prayer is annulled by a dog, a donkey and a woman (if they pass in front of the praying people)." Vol. 1, Book 9, Number 490	Bible is silent.
Troublesome house flies	**Troublesome house flies**
"The prophet (Mohammed) said, 'If a house fly falls in the drink of any one of you, he should dip it (in the drink), for one of its wings has a disease and the other has the	Bible is silent on this matter.

Islam says:	The Bible says:
cure for the disease.' " Hadith, Vol.4, Book 54, Number 537	
Penalty for keeping a dog as a pet	**Penalty for keeping a dog as a pet**
"Allah's apostle (Mohammed) said, 'If somebody keeps a dog, he loses one Qirat (of the reward) of his good deeds everyday, except if he keeps it for the purpose of agriculture or for the protection of livestock.' " Hadith, Vol. 4, Book 54, Number 541	No penalty for having a family pet.
Ban on killing snakes in houses	**Ban on killing snakes in houses**
"Ibn 'Umar used to kill snakes, but when Abu Lubaba informed him that the prophet (Mohammed) had forbidden the killing of snakes living in houses, he gave up killing them.' " Hadith, Vol. 4, Book 54, Number 530	Bible is silent.
Exception for certain snakes	**Exception for certain snakes**
"The prophet (Mohammed) ordered that a short-tailed or mutilated-tailed snake (i.e. Abtar) should be killed, for it blinds the on-looker and causes abortion." Hadith, Vol. 4, Book 54, Number 528 "The prophet (Mohammed) said, 'Kill the snake with two white lines on its back, for it blinds the on-looker and causes abortion.' " Hadith, Vol. 4 Book 54, Number 527	Not in the Bible.
Salamanders	**Salamanders**
"Narrated Um Sharik: That the prophet (Mohammed) ordered	Bible is silent.

Islam says:	The Bible says:
her to kill Salamanders." Hadith, Vol. 4, Book 54, Number 526	
Jinns (genies) and rats	**Jinns (genies) and rats**
"The prophet (Mohammed) said, 'Cover your utensils and tie your water skins, and close your doors and keep your children close to you at night, as the Jinns (evil spirits) spread out at such time and snatch things away. When you go to bed, put out your lights, for the mischief-doer (i.e. the rat) may drag away the wick of the candle and burn the dwellers of the house.' " Hadith, Vol. 4, Book 54, Number 533	Bible is silent.
People turning into rats	**People turning into rats**
"The prophet (Mohammed) said, 'A group of Israelites were lost. Nobody knows what they did. But I do not see them except that they were cursed and changed into rats, for if you put the milk of a she-camel in front of a rat, it will not drink it, but if the milk of a sheep is put in front of it, it will drink it.' " Hadith, Vol. 4, Book 54, Number 524	No such thing in the Bible.
Satan in the nasal passages	**Satan in the nasal passages**
"Narrated Abu Huraira: The prophet (Mohammed) said, 'If anyone of you rouses from sleep and performs the ablution, he should wash his nose by putting water in it and then blowing it out thrice, because Satan has stayed in the upper part of his nose	Bible is silent.

Islam says:	The Bible says:
all the night.' " Hadith, Vol. 4, Book 54, Number 516	
Spitting to stop bad dreams	**Spitting to stop bad dreams**
"Narrated Abu Qatada: The prophet (Mohammed) said, 'A good dream is from Allah, and a bad or evil dream is from Satan; so if anyone of you has a bad dream of which he gets afraid, he should spit on his left side and should seek refuge with Allah from its evil, for then it will not harm him.' " Hadith, Vol. 4, Book 54, Number 513	Bible is silent.
Proper way to spit in the mosque	**Proper way to spit in the mosque**
"The prophet saw some sputum in the direction of the Qibla (on the wall of the mosque) and he disliked that and the sign of disgust was apparent from his face. So he got up and scraped it off with his hand and said, 'Whenever anyone of you stands for the prayer, he is speaking in private to his Lord or his Lord is between him and his Qibla. So, none of you should spit in the direction of the Qibla, but one can spit to the left or under his foot.' The prophet (Mohammed) then took the corner of his sheet and spat in it and folded it and said, 'Or you can do like this.' " Hadith, Vol. 1, Book 8, Number 399	Bible is silent.

ISLAM — the books

The books of Islam are the Koran, which has 114 chapters or suras, and the Haddith, which is in several volumes. Mohammed was illiterate and could write nothing. He began having visions of a being which claimed to be the angel Gabriel.

Mohammed told other people, who wrote down what he said. Those writings are the 114 chapters of the Koran. After Mohammed died many people related things which he had done and said, and these were all written down and make up the various volumes of the Haddith.

The entire religion of Islam rests on the word of one illiterate Arab man who lived in the desert in the 7th century.

Chapter 6

Freemasonry: A Counterfeit Religion
by Alan Franklin

"Have no fellowship with the unfruitful works of darkness, but rather reprove them."

Ephesians. 5:11

"Wherefore come out from among them, and be ye separate, saith the Lord, and touch not the unclean thing; and I will receive you"

2 Corinthians 6:17

Freemasonry says:	The Bible says:
God is called The Great Architect of The Universe. However, the greatest secret of Masonry is that the "true" name of God is Ja-Bul-On. Ja is from the Hebrew word for Jehovah, Bul from Baal, the sun god, and On is from the god Osiris of the Egyptian mystery religion. This is the unholy trinity of Freemasonry.	God is The Father. Jesus said: "I am the way, the truth and the life: no man cometh to the Father, but by Me." John 14:6
All gods are accepted by Freemasonry.	"Thou shalt have no other gods before Me. Thou shalt not bow down thyself to them nor serve them." Exodus 20: 3–5
The lodge is for men of good reputation	Christ came to save sinners 1 Timothy 1:15.

Freemasonry says:	**The Bible says:**
The secrets of Freemasonry are sealed on oath and must never be revealed on pain of having one's throat cut, tongue torn out by the roots and their body buried in the sand at low-water mark	The Lord Jesus said: "I spake openly to the world… and in secret have I said nothing." John 18:20. He told us to swear no oaths but let our yes be yes and our no be no.
The Masonic "all-seeing eye" is the eye of Osiris, the ancient god of Egypt. "Everything good in nature comes from Osiris-order, harmony, and the favourable temperatures of the seasons and celestial periods." Albert Pike, *Morals and Dogmas of the Ancient and Accepted Scottish rite of Freemasonry.*	God doesn't have one eye! Osiris was just another false deity.
The head of each Masonic Lodge is called The Worshipful Master.	A Christian could not use this title: our only master is the Lord Jesus Christ, and a man cannot serve two masters.
At each initiation ceremony the apprentice Mason is told that he is in darkness and needs to go into the light. His introduction into masonry is described as a "new birth". *Mackey's Masonic Ritualist*, p. 24.	The Lord Jesus is the light of the world! All Christians are born again when they accept the Lord Jesus Christ. Unless a man is born again he cannot enter the kingdom of God (John 3:3–7). This is the only new birth that is possible.
At this ceremony each new Mason is given a lambskin to wear, in which he is buried. He is told that after death he will be judged, while wearing the lambskin, at the Great White Throne judgement.	This white throne judgement is for sinners only! (Revelation 20). This is a judgement of the damned. Matthew 7:15 warns of false prophets who come in sheep's clothing.
Masons claim their movement started with King Solomon. In fact it began in 1717. (Source: *The Encyclopedia Britannica*.)	The Lord Jesus is from everlasting to everlasting.

Freemasonry says:	The Bible says:
In the 17th degree Masons are given a secret password to get them into heaven on death. This word is Abaddon.	Abaddon is the Hebrew name of the chief demon who rules over the Abyss, one of the four sections of Sheol (the underworld). He is the "angel of the bottomless pit." Revelation 9:11. Satan makes fools of those who follow him, and leads them on a pied piper walk to Hell. In Greek this evil being is called Apollyon.

Would you join a club that you knew nothing about? Would you then allow a noose to be put round your neck, roll up your left trouser leg and be led blindfold three times round a Masonic lodge building? Would you then go through a vile, degrading ceremony in which you become a Freemason and promise to never reveal masonry's secrets, on pain of having your throat cut, tongue torn out and your body buried in the sand at low water mark? This is the humiliation that Entered Apprentice masons submit themselves to, in the belief that they are entering some sort of fraternity which will help them in business or their careers. But there is a terrible, eternal price to pay for these naïve newcomers. Masons call Freemasonry "The Craft." In fact it is witchcraft.

What does God's word say about secret oaths? "But I say , unto you swear not at all; neither by heaven; for it is God's throne; nor by the earth; for it is His footstool... but let your communication be, yea, yea; nay, nay; for whatsoever is more than these cometh of evil" *(Matthew 5:34–37)*. So let your yes be yes and your no be no — swear no oaths! It could not be plainer. The oaths taken by Entered Apprentice, Second (Fellowcraft) and Third Degree (Master Mason) Freemasons all contain bloodcurdling threats to those who violate the oaths and obligations. Yet all end "so help me God." But God has no part in any of these sick ceremonies. For it is not the God of the Bible being invoked. This is a secret society with secret meetings, secret codes, secret signs, handshakes and symbols. The more you learn about it — which is what most low level masons never do — you realize that it has much to be secret about. Remember, the Lord Jesus came for everyone — not self-selected groups of men meeting behind closed doors.

The oaths taken by those in the first three degrees bind the mason to his fellow masons, in such a way that he has to give them help and preference. So a Christian who got involved through ignorance could not be open and honest, for example praying frankly with his wife or fellow believers, because they are excluded from the inner circle of masonry, whose alleged secrets must be kept. But the Bible says we should not be linked with unbelievers. "Be ye not unequally yoked together with unbelievers: for what fellowship hath righteousness with unrighteousness? And what communion hath light with darkness?" (*2 Corinthians 6:14*). In the final Blue Lodge degree, the Master Mason candidate is laid out as if dead and the Worshipful Master of the lodge symbolically raises him from the dead. A similar initiation takes place in other occult societies, for example Skull and Bones, to which the Bush ex-presidents belong. It is a blasphemous tilt at the resurrected Jesus. He alone can raise people from death!

It is true that many rich, famous and titled people have been and are Freemasons. Members of the Royal Family, for example, although not Prince Charles. So what? Do they know the Lord Jesus? Men's opinions are not important — and that includes mine. It is the words of the Bible, faith in the Lord Jesus and the truth, as opposed to falsehood, that we should seek out. For the truth will set you free. Jesus is "the Truth." Freemasonry is based on a lie. Satan is the "Father of Lies." Secrecy and ignorance are tools he wields — tools like the masons' tools which symbolize Freemasonry. I have known a number of Freemasons and most are unremarkable men, no worse and no better than most of us. However, this doesn't apply to masonry, which shields its darkest secrets from the naïve majority in the Blue Lodge — the first three degrees, which is as far as most Freemasons progress.

As masons move through the degrees of "The Craft", the oaths increase in bloodthirstiness and unpleasantness, becoming darker and more demonic in tone. The Entered Apprentice, the learner Freemason, is told during his initiation ceremony: "Having been kept for a considerable time in a state of darkness, what in your present situation is the predominant wish of your heart?" The candidate replies: "Light." Masonry teaches that it brings its new members into the light and that a new mason journeys from darkness into light. This is a parody of Christianity, and although Freemasons will claim that many members are Christians, these men are deluded, for they are following the false god of a false religion.

Religion? That's what they call it. The authoritative *Coil's Masonic*

Encyclopedia states *(p. 158)*. "Freemasronry is undoubtedly a religion." Many other masonic writers echo this. Masonry teaches that salvation is through "good works." Masons meet in lodges under the all-seeing eye of Horus, the son (in legend) of Osiris and Isis. His right eye was white, representing the sun, his left black and representing the moon. In mythology Horus lost his left eye in battle with his evil brother, Seth. Seth tore out the eye, but lost the fight. The eye was magically renewed by Thoth, the god of writing, the moon, and magic. Horus presented his eye to Osiris, who experienced rebirth in the underworld. So this is a pagan god watching the antics of masons. It is also an occult symbol found in many other places of spiritual darkness. Candidates taking the 17th degree (Knights of the East and West) learn a "sacred word," Abaddon. If you turn to Revelation 9:11 you can see that Abaddon is the demonic angel who is king over the demons of the bottomless pit.

There are numerous such clues, many masonic writings, which confirm the occult, demonic nature of Freemasonry. Leading masonic writer Albert Pike gave the game away by stating that Lucifer is god! "If Lucifer were not God, would Adonay (the Christian God) whose deeds prove his cruelty, perfidy and hatred of man, barbarism and repulsion for science, would Adonay and his priests calumniate him? Yes, Lucifer is God, and unfortunately Adonay is also god. For the eternal law is that there is no light without shade- no white without black, for the absolute can only exist as two gods..." (**Albert Pike***, Grand Commander, Sovereign Pontiff of Universal Freemasonry, July 14 1889 —Instructions to the 23 Supreme Councils of the World.*) This concept of darkness and light explains the white/black tile pattern in lodges. In fact Freemasonry is as far from Christianity as black is from white.

You cannot be an atheist and a mason; you cannot proclaim "Jesus is Lord" in the lodge, but you can be a Hindu, Buddhist or Muslim as long as you believe in "The Supreme Architect of The Universe." This is the name masons are first told is the name of God. Men drawn into the lodge because they think it will give them contacts in business, or advance their careers, usually have little knowledge of Christianity or any other religion. So they accept that men of all religions worship the same god, but that he has a variety of different names. Any supreme being will do. This sounds reasonable as long as you don't know the truth.

Modern Freemasonry began in 1717, but many of its practices, handshakes, symbols and signs date back to ancient Egypt — perhaps even to Babylon, source and inspiration for all false religion. While at the lower levels Freemasons may think they belong to a men's fellowship, a good club with useful business contacts, at the highest levels are those who believe they are guardians of ancient secrets, "The Mysteries," involving ritual magic, the fate of nations — and the building of a New World Order. (**Albert Pike**, *Morals and Dogma of the Ancient and Accepted Scottish Rite of Freemasonry.*)

We will now shine some light into the dark corners of the lodge, starting with a rebuttal of the lie above. *Isaiah 45:5* states: "I am the Lord, and there is none else, there is no god beside me." All other "gods" are idols or demons. If you give them equal status with the Lord Jesus, then you are contradicting God and are damned. The white throne judgment that Freemasons value so highly is in fact a judgment of the damned *(Rev 20:11–15)*! The foundation of Freemasonry, that all men who believe in a deity worship God, is false and anti-Christian. Does Freemasonry say Jesus Christ is the only way to salvation *(John 14:6)*? The answer is clearly no, which contradicts the whole basis of scripture. The Holy Bible is in lodges — but only as an item of decoration. If masons read it, they would see that they are in a false religious system, one that teaches that salvation is through "good works." (This is condemned in *Ephesians 2:8–10)*.

One glance at a Freemasons' lodge should tell you all you need to know about this dark force in society. I have sought out many and they are invariably sinister looking places, often with windows blanked out. You cannot walk in and look around — they are locked, and, when meetings take place, guarded by the Tyler at the door. The Tyler is appointed by the Worshipful Master or elected by the members of the Lodge. He is charged with examining the Masonic credentials of anyone wishing to enter the Lodge, keeping unqualified persons from infiltrating masonic meetings and admitting only those qualified *(**Source**, Wikipedia)*. Masonry is a secret society. Contrast this with all Christian churches, even bad ones; even lukewarm ones! Anybody is welcome, all can go in and, in most at least, you will be welcomed. It's a different spirit. There are no secrets in sound Christian churches.

There was a brave and powerful exposé of Freemasonry on TV in Britain in 2008, when Jack Harris, a former worshipful master of a masonic lodge, was a guest on the John Ankerberg show. Mr. Harris said that in his masonic days he taught new masons that the name of God could be any god of any religion — not exclusively the name of Jesus Christ, in whom all deity dwells. In masonry the gods of all religions are acceptable, and some of the new masons would swear with their hand on the Koran or on the Vedas.

In the first degree the mason wore a white lambskin apron, in which he would be buried. The apron is the badge of a mason. Said Jack Harris: "I taught that by the purity of his life and conduct he will gain entrance into the celestial lodge above, where the Supreme Architect of the Universe resides. But the Word of God tells us in Ephesians 2:8, 9 that it is by grace we are saved through faith, not through works lest anyone should boast. So I taught that man a lie."

He said that in the 3rd degree of masonry he taught the legend of Hiram Abiff, that as he took the tools of the builders' trade and applied moral truths of masonry, he would build the spiritual temple of his body, so when he was raised up, he would be accepted into the "lodge above." Mr. Harris added: "But the Word of God says it is only through the shed blood of Jesus Christ, through His sacrifice at Calvary, that we can gain entry to heaven." He said the mason he taught might have gone to hell.

This one-time "Worshipful Master" taught the masons to keep everything they learned in the lodge secret, because it was designed for those found worthy by Freemasonry. "But God says no one is worthy. Romans 3:10 says there is none righteous, not even one. In Freemasonry you are found worthy through their ritual, their creed, their virtuous education." But he pointed out that the Bible said salvation was a free gift and that to gain eternal life, you must ask as a child.

Mr Harris also pointed people to Ephesians 5:11: "Have no fellowship with the unfruitful works of darkness, but rather reprove them." He said all the teachings of Freemasonry add up to salvation by works, and as believers we are commanded to have no fellowship with these doctrines. He challenged any Freemasons who might be watching the program: "Can you truthfully in your heart embrace these teachings (of the masons) and still say 'I'm being obedient to the Word of God and the Lord Jesus Christ?' It is time to decide."

Most masons stay in the Blue Lodge, as a third degree Master Mason. If you want to go further it costs you, as the degrees become expensive. Many degrees are bought with no study involved, which is one explanation of why Freemasons often know little of the organization they have pledged to support. Freemasons have a choice of advancement through the Scottish Rite, which ends with the 32nd degree, or the degree of Knights Templar in the York Rite, which has ten degrees and is for those who profess to be Christians. If you reach the 32nd degree, you can get the honorary 33rd degree and become a Shriner, as can a Knights Templar. My father became a Shriner, a member of the Mystic

Shrine, wearing a red fez and pledging an oath to Allah on the Koran, before an Islamic shrine.

Shriners are the public face of Freemasonry in North America, riding on motorcycles in parades, staging Shrine circuses and generally having a good time. They shower carnival onlookers with thousands of little charms — eastern charms. Islamic charms. For the Shrine is Islamic Freemasonry. Its full title is The "Ancient Arabic Order, Nobles of The Mystic Shrine." The fez they wear has an interesting history. In the 8th century Muslims overran the Moroccan city of Fez shouting: "There is no god but Allah and Muhammed is his prophet." They then slaughtered 50,000 Christians, men, women and children, and the streets ran red with their blood. The Islamics dipped their fez hats in this blood, staining them red. That's why Shriners' hats are red. Blood red. The blood of Christians. There are very few Christians in Morocco today. But there are a lot of Shriners whooping it up in America, Canada and elsewhere.

Many Shriners seem ignorant of what they have committed themselves to: a blasphemous religion that will send them straight to hell unless they leave and repent. The vile oath they take should tell any who join the shrine temple all they need to know. The penalty includes "having my eyeballs pierced to the center with a three edged blade, my feet flayed, and... may Allah, the god of Arab, Moslem and Mohammedan, the god of our fathers, support me to the entire fulfillment of the same, amen, amen, amen." (*The Ancient Arabic Order, Nobles of The Mystic Shrine,* 35-39, Allen Publishing Co, NY, NY). If you turn to the color pages in this book you will see a picture we took in Springfield, Missouri, when the Shriners were having a Shrine circus for local children. The Shriner we spoke to outside the building claimed to be a Christian. But every facet of this false faith, every sign on their building, screams the opposite. Across the top was an elaborate Eastern-looking dome with Arabic writing on it. What did the writing say, we asked one of the Shriners. He told us it was "just for decoration."

We took a picture of it and sent it to the Middle East, where Arab Christians translated it. The words read: "There is no god but Allah." A Christian Shriner? I also pictured the words on the foundation stone. They read: "Abou Ben Adhem Shrine Mosque A.A.O.N.M.S. 1922." So the Shriners' building is even called a mosque. Can these men be so blind they do not read the inscription on their own foundation stone? Words mean something. Incidentally, if you call the Abou Ben Adhem shrine mosque you can ask for a being called "the potentate." There is another man with the title "high priest and prophet." Can you imagine men accepting such puffed-up descriptions? The Bible tells us there is only one potentate, the Lord Jesus.

"...who is the blessed and only Potentate, the King of kings and Lord of lords."   1 Timothy 6:15

The full title of the Shrine is the Ancient Arabic Order of the Nobles of the Mystic Shrine (A.A.O.N.M.S.), and it was "founded in New York City in 1872 by Billy Florence, an actor, and Walter Fleming, a physician. In the beginning, Fleming and Florence realized it needed a colorful, exciting backdrop. As the legend goes, Fleming attended a party in Marseilles, France, hosted by an Arabian diplomat. At the end of the party, the guests became members of a secret society. Florence realized this might be the ideal vehicle for the new fraternal body, and he made copious notes and drawings of the ceremony. When Florence returned to the States, Fleming agreed and together they created the elaborate rituals, designed the emblem and costumes, and formalized the salutation. Though the Shrine is not itself a secret society, it still retains much of the mysticism and secrecy of its origins." (Source: *www.abashrine. com* — the website of *the Shriners of Springfield, MO.*) It is true that "Shriners do a lot of good." But they do it ostentatiously, with the maximum hoopla and promotion of the fact.

What did the Lord Jesus say about giving? Do your charity in secret! Don't wave around "big" checks — often big in physical size only — and demand that the newspaper photograph you "doing good". Be discreet, be anonymous, and God, who sees all things, will see you get your reward. But it won't be in the Shriners' Lodge... Here's how the King James Bible puts it:

"Take heed that ye do not your alms before men, to be seen of them: otherwise ye have no reward of your Father which is in heaven.

"Therefore when thou doest thine alms, do not sound a trumpet before thee, as the hypocrites do in the synagogues and in the streets, that they may have glory of men. Verily I say unto you, they have their reward.

"But when thou doest alms, let not thy left hand know what thy right hand doeth;

That thine alms may be in secret: and thy Father which seeth in secret Himself shall reward thee openly."

Matthew 6:1–4

I am not convinced that a high percentage of Masonic giving goes to anything other than helping Masons and Masons' widows, or on having a good time at conventions. Various exposés, which it is not my purpose to go into here, have questioned the allegedly wonderful works of Freemasonry. Furthermore, Masons work against those they dislike or who are in conflict or competition with masonic-run businesses. I have personal experience of this, and when I ran a small business I found that competing against Masons was impossible in some towns. When the situation changed and our business was bought out, the former leading Freemason who had been the cause of our problems took me out to lunch, made me a job offer and said that all doors would be open if I joined the lodge. I did not want to join such people. I declined.

As a newspaper editor I also invariably had unpleasant, rather threatening messages if I presumed to criticize their so-called "craft". They were certainly crafty in trying to suppress criticism. They most certainly did not "love their enemies," as our Lord commanded. Master Masons swear not to cheat each other. No mention is made of the rest of society. We journalists were aware that prior to a Mayor being selected in various cities, the candidates were first selected at lodge meetings. This cut across party lines. I have also reported on criminal trials where masonic signals flashed around the courtroom. Masons are strongly represented in the law, the police and the army. The reader will be able to work out what this means for fair and equal justice for all. Even Christians fully aware of the evils of masonry have said to me privately that they were tempted to join the lodge just to get an "in" on local business.

There was one good outcome in that the Mason I referred to above came into a church I once attended, sat next to me and repented in tears for his many sins (he was a homosexual, among other things). So it is possible, even at an advanced age, to come out from the darkness of the lodge into the light of the Lord. The same man was also a sidesman — usher — in the Anglican church (Episcopalians) and many Anglicans in Britain, including numerous clergymen, are in the lodge. Other men who were once Masons, but saw the real light — the Lord Jesus Christ — have a good website called *emfj.org* — ex-masons for Jesus. They put it this way: "Would Christians substitute the name GAOTU (Great Architect Of The Universe) for God and do away with the name of Jesus so that pagans could join with them in prayer without being offended? No, Christians would have shared Jesus with the pagans so that they too might have salvation through faith in Him.

"It is true that there is one God. However, all men, specifically pagans, do not worship that one God. The worshippers of Baal learned the truth on Mt. Carmel. Baal is not the God of Abraham, Isaac and Jacob. Judgment was swift on Mt. Carmel. (See 1 Kings 18:20–40.) The god of Freemasonry, the GAOTU, is also not the God of the Bible. Will God judge Masons who do not repent and continue to worship the GAOTU any differently than he judged the worshippers of Baal?"

Know ye not that the unrighteous shall not inherit the kingdom of God? Be not deceived: neither fornicators, nor **idolaters**, nor adulterers, nor effeminate, nor abusers of themselves with mankind, nor thieves, nor covetous, nor drunkards, nor revilers, nor extortioners, shall inherit the kingdom of God *(1 Cor 6:9–10)*.

Here's how the born-again ex-Masons reach out to their former associates:

"What will Jesus tell the Mason who claims to be a Christian? Not every one that saith unto me, Lord, Lord, shall enter into the kingdom of heaven; but he that doeth the will of my Father which is in heaven. Many will say to me in that day, Lord, Lord, have we not prophesied in thy name? and in thy name have cast out devils? and in thy name done many wonderful works? And then will I profess unto them, I never knew you: depart from me, ye that work iniquity." *(Matthew 7:21–23)*

"By joining in pagan worship ceremonies, WE sinned against God. When we realized that the GAOTU was not the God of the Bible, we claimed the promise found in John's first letter: 'This is the message we have heard from him and declare to you: God is light; in Him there is no darkness at all. If we claim to have fellowship with Him yet walk in the darkness, we lie and do not live by the truth. But if we walk in the light, as He is in the light, we have fellowship with one another, and the blood of Jesus, His Son, purifies us from all sin. If we claim to be without sin, we deceive ourselves and the truth is not in us. **If we confess our sins, He is faithful and just and will forgive us our sins and purify us from all unrighteousness.'**

"If you are a Christian who has become ensnared in Freemasonry, we urge you to confess your involvement in Freemasonry as sin and renounce it, as we have. Jesus wants to forgive you, but his forgiveness is dependant on your confession and repentance" *(Ex-Masons for Jesus)*.

Freemasonry is a pagan religion. Paul warned that it was not possible for a man to participate in paganism and also be a Christian. He wrote:

"Ye cannot drink the cup of the Lord and the cup of devils:

ye cannot be partakers of the Lord's table and of the table of devils." 1 Corinthians 10:21

In John 4:24, Jesus told us: "God is a Spirit: and they that worship Him must worship Him in spirit and in truth."

If a man has bought into the masonic lie that all men worship the same god, simply using a variety of different names, then he cannot be worshipping in truth. Therefore, he cannot be worshipping God when he goes into the lodge. But he is worshipping something, hidden under the humiliating mumbo jumbo that no grown man should submit to.

Christians have no place in the lodge or shrine, and Shriners and Masons have no place in the local church. Our daughter and son-in-law live on the slopes of Mount Carmel, where Elijah confronted 450 prophets of Baal and 400 other false prophets. He laid out two options:

"How long halt you between two opinions? If the Lord be God, follow Him. But if Baal, then follow him" 1 Kings 18:21

There is a choice to be made. Choose this day who you will serve!

Chapter 7

Table of Truth: Evolution vs. the Bible
by Pat Franklin

"The heavens declare the glory of God."

Psalm 19:1

"The fool says in his heart, 'There is no god.' "

Psalm 14:1

Once upon a time, millions and millions of years ago, there was a little bitty thing, smaller than the head of a pin. Suddenly there was a big bang and the little thing flew in all directions. Bits of it expanded and got very hot and became billions of stars. Other bits were flung everywhere and became planets and moons. Then it started to rain with lots of lightning, for millions of years, on one rocky, empty planet called Earth. Terrible weather back then. Some primeval soup started sloshing around. One day a little blob of slime started to crawl up out of the soup. Before you know it, a few million more years went by and soon the whole planet was filled with an amazing variety of all sorts of intricate living creatures, including us.

That's your story for tonight, dear; now go to sleep.

That is a particularly stupid fairy tale, I am sure you will agree. It would not have kept my kids entertained, but it keeps massed ranks of academics happy the world over. As for me, I outgrew fairy stories long ago.

Even as an out and out liberal totally opposed to Christianity, I did not believe in evolution. It is just so downright dumb. A child could see through it. Scientists are increasingly questioning it these days, as it is not even scientific. First of all, in nature something does not come from nothing, as indeed the First Law of Thermodynamics declares (matter and energy are constant and cannot be created or destroyed). Of course this takes no account of God, who has no problem creating something from nothing. Then there is the Second Law of Thermodynamics, with the concept of entropy, which includes the idea that everything deteriorates over time, whereas evolution theory says that simple organisms form themselves into ever more complex and orderly arrangements. The Second Law was so devastating for evolutionary theory that they are now changing the concept of entropy to fit in with evolution, claiming that order comes from disorder.

Animals do not turn into other animals, no matter how much time you give them. It doesn't happen; it never happened; it is impossible. That is why there are no transitional fossils. Selective breeding, yes, that is scientific fact obviously, but that is *not* evolution. Selective breeding uses the genetic information that exists and selects for certain traits. In evolution, new information is assumed to be added, but there is no mechanism in our cells to add information to DNA. So they have a problem. Species mutating into other species? Don't be ridiculous! That is science fiction, and third rate science fiction at that.

Darwin was convinced that one species could gradually change into another, but he was a Victorian. He lived before knowledge exploded and scientists found out more about how nature really operates. Darwin had no electron microscope, and had never heard of DNA. As Jacob Prasch once said, one nucleus of one cell is far more complicated than the entire electrical system of the space shuttle. Darwin was ignorant of the incredible complexity of our biology. The more scientists find out, the more they realize there is to find out.

Our DNA, the double helix in each cell of our body, replicates itself when the cell splits. It is a code, a language, an information system which determines our characteristics. There is no mechanism for adding new information, but information can be damaged or lost. So if, when we are forming in our mother's womb, we have DNA coded for two arms, we get two arms. If that code gets jumbled or changed, we are in trouble. Mutations *can* be harmless, but they are never good news. Evolutionists cannot come up with one example of a good mutation. Yet the theory of evolution is built on the supposition that over a long enough period of time, there would be mutations changing one species into another, always adding information, always increasing in complexity and advancing to more and better life forms. It just does not happen and it did not happen. I wonder what an evolutionist would do if he learned that the baby in his wife's womb had a mutation in its genes. I think he would be panicking like mad, trying to find out if the baby was badly damaged. He would not be rejoicing that the race was making a great leap forward.

Evolutionists point to the "record of the rocks," the millions of fossils, but the "record" doesn't exist. The fossils do not show creatures gradually changing into new species. They show that each species was just there, fully formed and perfect, with no incremental, slow changes and no "halfway" creatures.

The witty creationist Dr. Kent Hovind was speaking at a conference which we attended in Pennsylvania in 2002. He told us that at one debate at an American college, an academic had said: "How can you expect us to believe that 270 (or however many) breeds of dogs all came from just one pair of dogs that came out of the Ark?" Dr. Hovind replied: "You have a bigger problem than I have, because you believe that 270 breeds of dogs came from a rock." "We don't say that at all," objected the academic. "Oh, yes, you do," said Dr. Hovind, and he took them through the standard evolutionist's creed: big bang, millions of years, rain falling on rocks, primeval soup forming, slimy critter crawling out, millions more years, bingo — dogs from rocks! The academic slunk off to drown his sorrows in some primeval soup.

It just didn't happen that way, my friends. What did happen is that in the beginning God created the heavens and the earth, just as He says in Genesis Chapter 1. Why is that so hard to believe? It makes a whole lot more sense than evolution. We do not have to apologise for believing what God says in His book. He did not make a mistake on the first page. The Creator knows how, when, where and why He made the first man and woman. We can rely absolutely on His word for what He did.

It is the evolutionists who have the problem, not us. No matter how many millions of years we paddle around in the sea, we are not going to grow any gills. And no matter how long we and our descendents might try flapping our arms, we are not going to sprout wings and fly. And if some unfortunate baby were to be born with feathers instead of arms, what a sad day, what a river of tears, what frantic searching for the best surgeon money can buy. Fortunately that will never happen, because our DNA does not contain the information needed for feathers to form, and there is no way nature can add information to our genes. Our genes can lose information, but not gain it. The fact that scientists today are messing with genetics and "creating" monstrosities does not prove evolution; it proves that men are yet again spitting in the face of God.

There's only one Creator and if you try to assume His role, it is going to bounce right back on you. God will not tolerate it for much longer.

Some evolutionists have outdone themselves when it comes to dinosaurs, theorising that the dinos could have evolved into birds. Oh. Stands to reason, doesn't it? They couldn't hack it as big guys, so maybe they started hunching down a little more each generation. And their scales (if they had scales) just started evolving into feathers. It was probably kind of itchy and uncomfortable for a few billion generations, and they had to have a lot of dino discipline to diet down from the size of a 10 story building to the sparrow in my garden. Come on, guys, you have got to be kidding! This is the best you can come up with? And they say **we're** gullible to believe in God? Oh, but now they say it was only the little bitty dinosaurs that turned into sparrows. Well, that won't wash either, I'm afraid. Each species of animal multiplies "after his kind", as Genesis Chapter 1 puts it. In other words, the breeding population of each species replicates its own DNA in its offspring and each breeding population grows after that particular "kind", just as Genesis Chapter 1 indicates. This entirely agrees with real science.

Our daughter came home from college one day saying that the biology students had come out of their class laughing. Someone asked them what was so funny. Evolution, they said. That day's class had been on evolution and they were all arguing against it and laughing at how stupid it appeared in the light of all they knew. These were not Christian students, far from it, but they had seen through the tissue of lies. They knew the emperor had no clothes on, and they were bold enough to say so! I wonder if they will be so brave and willing to stand up for truth if their jobs some day depend on whether or not they teach the lie of evolution?

What about the Great Flood? Truth or fiction? Absolute truth. Dr Farid Abou-Rahme, a consultant civil engineer who lives in Woking, Surrey, England, gave a convincing seminar at Surrey University on the subject of the Flood. Get his book *And God Said...* or, even better, invite him to speak. He does a series of seminars on creation, science, the Flood, and Noah's Ark, with a Powerpoint presentation, and his book has been translated into many languages.

The Flood makes sense of the world about us. Next time you take a trip, be on the lookout for evidence of the Flood. It is amazing what you see if you look, even if, like us, you have no specialized knowledge. On the Isle of Wight off the south coast of England, for example, there is a place called Alum Bay, famous for its colored sand (see our picture pages). The sandy cliffs are an amazing sight after a rainfall, when the colors stand out much more clearly. There is ochre, pink, gray, black, and yellow in great swatches, looking like God just painted a huge abstract mural. When we were there a few years back, the cliffs were behind a makeshift barrier. A sign warned tourists not to touch the fragile cliffs, because they are eroding. Funny, I would have thought that all those millions of years and all that rain falling would have long ago put paid to the crumbly cliffs, but no, somehow those delicate structures still stand. Ain't evolution wonderful? No, seriously, those beautiful cliffs have not been around for millions of years. They have stood resplendent since they were formed at the time of Noah's Flood, in about 4500 B.C.

If you walk along the beach at the foot of those wonderful cliffs, you will see lots of chunks of the colored mineral sands which constantly break off and roll down on to the beach. We're not sure if you're allowed to pick them up these days, or if "Mother Earth" would be offended and some court would slap a fine on you. A shop there sells containers of the sand, layered in multi-colored stripes. We have one to show anyone who is interested in God's incredible creation. It is a souvenir of Noah's Flood.

If any reader happens to be going to Alum Bay, there is another interesting sight to see nearby. We walked up the road past the old fort and looked at the brilliant white chalk cliffs in the distance. They contain neat horizontal rows of dark spots which we could make out through the binoculars. I wondered if they could be chunks of flint laid neatly in layers as each tide swept in, depositing new material during the Flood. There are similar formations along the A3 highway in England, white cliffs with lines of black dots running through them. They are certainly all leftovers from the Flood.

We saw the same phenomenon in northern Israel, just by the border with Lebanon, at a place called Rosh Ha Nikra. There we were able to get close enough to touch the cliffs and take photos. The stunning white cliffs look in places like they were just extruded from a giant mixer, and there, arranged neatly in rows, were the same horizontal lines of black rocks. I just laughed with delight when I saw them. To me they are like a billboard from God that says something like: "Look, guys, here is some more proof; I'll put it in black and white so you can't miss it this time." It is just so obvious that the cliffs were made as the Flood mixed and blended earth and water, sand and sea creatures, all of it in a gigantic swirling blend that slopped around with each tidal movement, and sloshed over when dry land started appearing. With each tide, a great mass of material would be swept around and deposited, and the heavier rocks would have sunk to the bottom, forming those neat rows. Then another tide comes in and deposits another load of material on top of yesterday's deposit. Once again, the black heavy rocks sink to the bottom of that day's sandy deposit, and another row of black dots stretches out along the coast. Those black dots are like Morse code and the translation is: "Here is more proof; the Flood was real; the Bible is true history; just open your eyes and use your noodle for a change."

Next time you go on vacation somewhere, watch for cliffs and rocks, look at how the land is formed; see if you can find some new Flood evidence. I think God loves it when we do this. It gives Him glory when you believe what He has written about the history of earth, His special planet.

By the way, did you ever stop to think that the word "pre-historic" is itself a lie? There is no such thing as pre-history. God tells us the history of the whole universe, from Day One, or as much as He cares to divulge at this time. As Dave Hunt points out, we know its history — who made it (God) and how He made it (with words, by speaking) and even why (God so loved...). He made it even though He knew what we would be like and all that would happen, but He loved it anyway, and He loves us anyway.

Also, Adam might well have been able to write, so forget the pre-history fairy tale. Apart from the Lord Jesus, he must have been the smartest man who ever lived, not some grunting caveman. He named every animal, and I am told that the Hebrew names actually describe the animals. The evolutionists think that with survival of the fittest, we are evolving into supermen and women. Upwards and onwards! The reverse is true — we have been going downhill ever since Adam sinned. People were much smarter then, with better genes. But over about six thousand years there have been so many damaging mutations that the race is sliding down a slippery slope. The mutations are destroying us, not "evolving" us into a superspecies.

Science now knows that Adam existed. A National Geographic Special, "DNA Mysteries: The Search for Adam," was aired in Britain in 2006. It followed the research of geneticist Spencer Wells. Wells was researching the Y chromosome, which only men have. It is passed from father to son. Following the track of particular mutations on the Y chromosome, Wells traced back to "super ancestors" who left their genetic imprint on huge numbers of men. These "super ancestors" were men like Genghis Khan, believed to have millions of descendents. Wells found that DNA samples of men around the world led back to various branches of "super ancestors" and that he was able to backtrack all the way to a single ancestor, one man whose particular mutation of the Y chromosome is found in every man alive today. He called this man "scientific Adam" and his research showed that he probably lived in east Africa 60,000 years ago. This program is absolutely fascinating; it is wonderful to see how true science points us to the Bible, not to Darwin.

But evolution is still true, you might say, because we are getting smarter all the time and we know so much more now. We know more because God has allowed knowledge to increase. The book of the prophet Daniel states in Chapter 12 verse 4: "But thou, O Daniel, shut up the words, and seal the book, even to the time of the end: many shall run to and fro, and knowledge shall be increased." This mainly refers to people in the last days trying to understand Bible prophecy, but it is a great definition of modern life — we *constantly* run to and fro and knowledge *has* increased. We are not getting smarter, but God has allowed us to have greater knowledge. Knowledge puffs up, and it certainly has puffed us up; we think we are really something. Apart from God's grace, we are nothing. We could not draw one more breath unless He allowed it.

As for cavemen, isn't it interesting that when the coming Great Tribulation devastates the earth, the great men (and women) end up hiding in caves and praying for the rocks to fall on them? God's little irony, perhaps.

One of the wonders of creation that strikes me as proof positive of the existence of God is the phenomenon of the total eclipse of the sun. This happens when the moon completely covers the sun. For a few moments the earth is darkened, and the sun is just a thin fiery circle round the edges of the dark moon. The fact that this can happen *ever*, at *all*, is completely incredible. When you think of the vast distances involved — 270,000 miles to the moon, 93 million miles to the sun — with our earth swinging round the sun, and the moon swinging round our earth, and, lo and behold, at certain times the moon is in *exactly* the right spot to completely cover the sun. It's impossible! And not only that, but it is *exactly* the right size to blot out the entire sun! Not one centimetre too big; not one centimetre too small; just the right size. If anyone could ever work out the probability of such a celestial event EVER happening, I would think the number would be greater than the universe itself. It is SO unlikely, so totally impossible that this should EVER take place! Yet it does. Once again, the heavens declare the glory of God!

We must make sure our children not only know the truth about creation, but that they are able to refute the lie of evolution. The evidence for creation is here — the incredibly intricate, perfect design of every creature, created by a Being who is infinitely more intelligent than we are. The evolutionists say it all came about by chance. Oh yeah, sure. Maybe those guys really did come from monkeys, because an intelligent man made in God's image could hardly believe such nonsense. It is just not reasonable. Take heart, folks. We do not have to apologize for believing Genesis literally; it makes perfect sense.

You would think that the scientists would have chucked Darwin and Co into a black hole by now, but no. A lot of them must know the truth, but they are not about to admit it. It might cost them their jobs, for a start. Also, the research grants would dry up, possibly for millions of years.

They surely had a wake up call when Mt. St. Helen's blew its top. I hope it blew some sense into some craniums, for it was like a science demonstration on a mega scale orchestrated by God to show everyone just exactly what power there is in His hand and what one explosion can do. I marvelled at one of the pictures in *Creation* magazine[1] showing a man standing in front of a cliff about 200 feet high, full of strata lines of the sort we are told took millions of years to be laid down — all formed in one afternoon when Mt. St. Helen's burped. I showed this awesome piece of evidence to a geography teacher. *He was not impressed!* Didn't I tell you we were going downhill? He must be one of those beings who descended from apes.

The science programs on British TV in recent years have been most interesting. One posed the question: "Where is the missing 96per cent of the universe?" Apparently it is now known that the universe should actually all fly apart, because there is not enough matter to provide the gravity to hold it all together. So they now have decided that there is about 75 per cent dark energy and about 20 per cent dark matter. We can't see, feel, hear or touch any of this hypothetical dark stuff, but they believe it's out there holding us all together. Wow. Then again, those guys could turn to Hebrews 1:3 and find out the truth, that the Lord Jesus is "upholding all things by the word of His power..." How amazing that the Lord had those words inserted in His book. He knew they would be needed in our day.

---

[1] Creation magazine, go to www.creation.com for an intellectual feast.

Another British program featured leading evolutionists and broadcasters giving dire warnings of a terrible danger facing our society, a danger so great that it could plunge us right back in the Dark Ages, causing the end of our civilization. The awful looming catastrophe is that some educators and scientists are actually talking seriously about the concept of Intelligent Design. Aarrgghh! Surely not! The next thing you know, they'll be believing in creation! The advice given in this program was: under no circumstances should scientists ever agree to a public debate on the question of Intelligent Design. This was their advice — don't debate! They are running scared, folks. They won't debate because they know they can't win. We had a term for this when I was growing up — scaredy cat. They have evolved into a bunch of scaredy cats!

One last point — bacteria. Evolutionists say that bacteria mutate quickly and that proves evolution. No. Please refer to the work of Dr. Jonathan Sarfati on the Creation Ministries International website *(creation.com),* particularly his article "Anthrax and antibiotics: Is evolution relevant?" Thank God for experts like Dr. Sarfati who not only know that the Bible is true, but can back it up with science.

I could go on and on about this, but there is a ton of information out there which is readily available. We get *Creation* magazine, which is excellent, and there is a more technical version of it for science buffs. Please subscribe, and get an extra subscription to lend or give away. It is full of readable articles, brilliant photos and graphics and lots of items for children and teens. We urge parents to get *Creation* magazine (www.creation.com) for their children, or for the Sunday School. Our daughter at one stage got her school to put a copy in the library. We have occasionally left copies at the doctor's office. Give a subscription to someone for Christmas or their birthday. What a great gift — the truth — there is nothing like it to fill your heart with joy.

If you are in Britain, there is also a permanent creation exhibition in a building on the seafront at Portsmouth, Hampshire. Called Genesis Expo, it is at 17 The Hard and admission is free. Some of the fossils for sale there come from the beach at Charmouth in Dorset. We once spent a happy few hours fossil hunting at Charmouth and our daughter Annie came away with a great ammonite — one of her souvenirs of Noah's Flood (see her ammonite on our picture pages). Happy rock-spotting! And just think — if you are a believer in the Lord Jesus, one day you will meet that wonderful man Noah, our distant relation. And rest assured — he was not descended from a monkey!

Our Table of Truth is below:

Evolution theory says:	The Bible says:
About 15 billion years ago, there was a point smaller than the head of a pin which contained all the matter and energy of the entire universe. It suddenly expanded, changing from a tiny spot to all the stuff of the universe, expanding outwards at great speed. This is known as the Big Bang.	In the beginning God created the heavens and the earth. Genesis 1:1 The Hebrew word *bara* (created) means created from nothing. God created everything from nothing.
You cannot possibly prove the existence of God.	"The heavens declare the glory of God; and the firmament shows His handiwork. Psalm 19:1 Nature itself, God's creation, is a proof of His existence. Did your car put itself together? Did your house build itself? No, nor did the universe just happen to spring into existence. The order in nature speaks clearly of a master Designer.
It took millions of years for all the gas of the Big Bang to coalesce and form planets etc.	"And the evening and the morning were the first day." Genesis 1:1. Day in Hebrew is yom and when it is preceded by a number it always means a 24 hour period. The context also proves that it is a literal 24 hours — "evening and morning".
Man is just an animal.	"And God said, Let us make man in our image, after our likeness: and let them have dominion... over all the earth." Genesis 1:26. Man is made in the image and likeness of God.
Millions of years ago our ancestors were swinging through the trees...	"And God said... have dominion... over every living thing that moves upon the earth." Genesis 1:28

Evolution theory says:	The Bible says:
	The first man did not swing in the trees; he had **dominion** over things that swing in trees.
Man is just an accident of time and chance.	"...for I am fearfully and wonderfully made: marvellous are Thy works..." Psalm 139:14
One species can evolve into something quite different.	"And God said, Let the earth bring forth the living creature **after his kind**... and it was so." Genesis 1:24 An ant cannot evolve into an elephant, a dog into a bear etc. Everything reproduces **after its kind**.
Life somehow came from non-living matter — from the rocks and gas that came out of the Big Bang. (This goes against the Law of Biogenesis in biology which states that life arises from life; it cannot come from non-living material. This basic law of biology was proven in 1864 by Louis Pasteur, but is discarded by anyone who believes in the Big Bang.)	"God formed man of the dust of the ground, and breathed into his nostrils the breath of life; and man became a living soul." Genesis 2:7
The earth was formed from a solar cloud consisting mainly of hydrogen. Under gravitation the cloud condensed and shrank to form the planets orbiting around the sun. The first rocks formed over 3,500 million years ago. Nothing was made by God.	"He stretches out the north over the empty place, and hangs the earth upon nothing." Book of Job 26:7 (Written about 2000 B.C., the oldest book in the Bible.) "And I saw another angel fly in the midst of heaven... saying with a loud voice, Fear God, and give glory to Him; for the hour of His judgement is come: and worship Him that made heaven, and earth, and the sea, and the fountains of

Evolution theory says:	The Bible says:
	waters." Revelation 14:7
There is no God.	"The fool says in his heart, 'There is no god.' " Psalm 14:1 and Psalm 53:1
Despite the evidence of intricate design in everything, there is no Designer; it all just developed over long periods of time.	"Beware lest any man spoil you through philosophy and vain deceit, after the tradition of men…" Colossians 2:8

Although the Bible is not a scientific textbook, where it does mention scientific facts, it is 100 per cent accurate. It has revealed many things that were unknown until modern times. For example:

- **Existence of land dinosaurs.** "Behemoth… he eats grass as an ox; he moves his tail like a cedar… his bones are like bars of iron… he is the chief of the ways of God… he lies in the coverts of the reed, and fens… the shady trees cover him with their shadow; the willows of the brook compass him about…he drinks up a river…" From the Book of Job, Chapter 40, verse 15 to end, the oldest book in the Bible, written about 2000 B.C. This was thought to be an elephant until fossilized dinosaur bones were discovered.
- **Existence of sea dinosaurs.** Leviathan, "None is so fierce that dare stir him up,.. he makes the deep to boil like a pot… upon earth there is not his like…" Book of Job. The whole of Chapter 41 contains the detailed description of this monster of the sea.
- **Continental drift and plate tectonics**. "…the name of one was Peleg (meaning division); for in his days was the earth divided…" Genesis 10:25. Written by Moses in about 1400 B.C. The theory that the earth had once been one land mass surrounded by water was not accepted by science until the 20th century. I remember articles in the better newspapers in England in the 1970s trying to prove that the continents had once been joined together.
- **The hydrologic (water) cycle.** "…the drops of water… pour down rain according to the vapour… which the clouds do drop and distil…" Job 36:27, 28. "All the rivers run into the sea, yet the sea is not full, unto the place from whence the rivers

come, thither they return again." Ecclesiastes 1:7, written by King Solomon in about 900 B.C.

- **Global air movement.** "The wind goes toward the south, and turns about to the north; it whirls about continually, and the wind returns again according to his circuits." Ecclesiastes 1:6,7, written by King Solomon in about 900 B.C.
- **The earth is round.** "…upon the circle of the earth." Isaiah 40:22, written about 760.
- **The earth is suspended in space.** "He stretches out the north over the empty place, and hangs the earth upon nothing." Job 26:7 (written about 2000 B.C., the oldest book in the Bible). Hindus, on the other hand, believed the earth was held up by four elephants standing on turtles.
- **The earth was made from things invisible.** Hebrew ll:3
- **Even time had a beginning.** "…evening and morning were the first day." Genesis 1:5
- **An expanding universe.** " which alone spreads out the heavens…" Job 9:8, written about 2000 B.C.; "who stretches out the heavens like a curtain." Psalm 102:4 (written about 1000 B.C.) "It is he that… stretches out the heavens as a curtain…" Isaiah 40:22; and "…the Lord thy maker, that hath stretched forth the heavens, and laid the foundations of the earth…" Isaiah 51:13 (written about 700 B.C.)
- **Mankind came from one man and one woman.** This has now been verified by extensive worldwide DNA tests. The tests show that all men share one particular gene on the Y chromosome, proving they are all descended from one particular man. In the case of women, tests show we are all descended from one particular woman, whom some call "Mitochondrial Eve."
- **It is impossible to count the stars.** "As the host of heaven cannot be numbered…" Jeremiah 33:22, written about 600 B.C.; but God knows how many, because: "He tells the number of the stars; He calls them all by their names." Psalm 147:4. People thought they could count the stars at one time, but God knew we would never be able to, and now the scientists know it too. An article in the *London Daily Telegraph* (July 23, 2003) estimated that there are ten times more stars in the night sky than grains of sand in the world's deserts and beaches — too many even for the most advanced computers to count.

- **Paths through the sea.** "...whatsoever passes through the paths of the seas." Psalm 8, a psalm of King David written about 1000 B.C. Our ships benefit greatly from the existence of ocean currents, including the Gulf Stream, a sort of conveyor belt crossing the Atlantic 40 miles wide and 2,000 feet deep.

Chapter 8

Table of Truth:
Mormon Church vs. the Bible

Founder: Joseph Smith in about 1830 in the U.S.A.
Also called: The Church of Jesus Christ of Latter-day Saints.
Foundational books: *Book of Mormon, Doctrines and Covenants, Pearl of Great Price, the Bible* (the first three are considered above the Bible and more accurate).
Headquarters: Salt Lake City, Utah.

Mormonism says:	The Bible says:
American Indians	**American Indians**
The *Book of Mormon* is the tale of a Jewish family who supposedly sailed from Israel to the Americas in about 600 B.C. According to the *Book of Mormon,* their descendents are the Indians.	DNA testing of 150 Indian tribes by Mormon scientists proves that the Indians have no Jewish blood.[1]
Marriage in heaven	**Marriage in heaven**
Mormon men will have wives in heaven.	No marriage in heaven. The Lord Jesus said: "For in the resurrection they neither marry, nor are given in marriage, but are as the angels of God in heaven." Matthew 22:30

[1] *"DNA vs. The Book of Mormon"* produced by Living Hope Ministries, 48 N. Main, Brigham City, Utah, 84302, USA.

Mormonism says:	The Bible says:
	"For when they rise from the dead, they neither marry, nor are given in marriage; but are as the angels which are in heaven." Mark 12:25
People living on the moon	**People on the moon**
There are tall people living on the moon, dressed like Quakers. This was actually taught by Joseph Smith, founder of the Mormons, as recorded by Oliver B. Huntington in his Journal, Vol. 3, p.166, kept at Utah State Historical Society. Huntington was told that he would be a missionary to the moon people. (Vol. 3, pp. 263–264). The Apollo moonshots failed to find any Quakers.	The writers of the Bible were inspired by the Holy Spirit, who knew very well that there was nothing on the moon but rocks and dust. Where the Bible does mention any scientific fact, it is always 100% accurate. There are many such facts in the Bible, written down hundreds and even thousands of years before science discovered them. (For example, that the earth is a sphere, hung on nothing — when many believed the world was flat. Isaiah 40:22; Job 26:7)
People living on the sun	**People living on the sun**
"So it is in regard to the inhabitants of the sun. Do you think it is inhabited? I rather think it is. Do you think there is any life there? No question of it; it was not made in vain." Brigham Young (*Journal of Discourses*, Vol. 13, p. 271).[2]	The Bible is silent.
Date of Christ's return	**Date of Christ's return**
On February 14, 1835, Joseph Smith prophesied that "…the	No man knows the day nor the hour, not even the angels in heav-

---

[2] *Journal of Discourses* is a 26 volume set of sermons by early Mormon leaders, "a rich mine of wealth" according to Apostle Orson Pratt. You can read it all online on http://www.journalofdiscourses.org.

Mormonism says:	The Bible says:
coming of the Lord, which was nigh even fifty-six years should wind up the scene." But Jesus did not come back in 1891. *The History of the Church*, Vol. 2, p. 182 (Salt Lake City, Utah: Deseret Book Co., 2nd ed. revised, 1976)	en. Matthew 24:36, Mark 13:32
Magic underwear	**Magic underwear**
Temple Mormons, the elite, are given "magic underwear" embroidered with Masonic symbols.	This is occult (demonic, the dark supernatural, sorcery). Occult magic is forbidden by the Bible. Chuck those occult undies on the bonfire! Ask the Lord Jesus to forgive you for this occult involvement and give Him your life today! (Deut. 18; Rev 21:8).
Peepstones	**Peepstones**
Joseph Smith used a peepstone, a stone with a hole in it to "peep" through, gazing into a hat, to magically translate the *Book of Mormon*, which was written on golden plates that subsequently disappeared.	"...wizards that mutter and peep..." Isaiah 8:19 "...these things are an abomination unto the LORD..." Deuteronomy 18:9–12 The use of peepstones or any other object for divination is occult, magic, forbidden by the Bible.
God the Father	**God the Father**
God was once a mortal man, but is now a resurrected man in heaven. "As man is, God once was. As God is, man can become." (*Mormon Doctrine* by Mormon theologian Bruce R. McConkie, from saying coined by 5th LDS president Lorenzo Snow in 1840.)	God is spirit. John 4:24 "God is not a man, that he should lie..." Numbers 23:19 "...from everlasting to everlasting, thou art God." Psalm 90:2

Mormonism says:	The Bible says:
"The Father has a body of flesh and bones as tangible as man's; the Son also." *Doctrines and Covenants* 130:22	"...a spirit does not have flesh and bones as you see that I have" Luke 24:39 Spirits do not have bodies. The Lord Jesus took on flesh when He became a man so that He could die for our sins.
God the Father became a god after learning truth and aggressively pursuing godhood. God has a wife and together they procreate spirit children.	"...before me there was no God formed, neither shall there be after me." Isaiah 43:10 There is no eternal mother in the Bible — only in witchcraft, New Age, and other false religions does a "mother" appear, e.g. Gaia, Mother Earth, Astarte, various fertility goddesses etc.
God the Father is Adam and is also Michael the Archangel "Hear, O inhabitants of the earth, ...our father Adam ...brought Eve, one of his wives... He is Michael the Archangel, the Ancient of Days... He is our Father and our God and the only God with whom we have to do. Every man upon the earth... must hear it. *Journal of Discourses* Vol. 1, pp. 50–51, Brigham Young, 1852	"And the LORD God formed man of the dust of the ground..." Genesis 2:7 God **made** Adam; He was **not** Adam; nor was He Michael the Archangel.
Achieving godhood	**Achieving godhood**
Man can become like God. "...then shall they be gods... because they have all power..." *Doctrines and Covenants* 132:20 "...they (believers) are gods..." *Doctrines and Covenants* 76:58 "... you have got to learn how to be gods yourselves..." Joseph Smith, *Journal of Discourses* 6:4	This was Satan's lie in the Garden of Eden "...ye shall be as gods..." Genesis 3:5 Man is God's creation, and we will never be equal with Him. Satan's downfall was his sin of pride, of wanting equality with God. "For thou (Lucifer) hast said in thine heart... I will be like

Mormonism says:	The Bible says:
and also from *Teachings of the Prophet Joseph Smith,* p.346 "The Lord created you and me for the purpose of becoming gods like Himself." Brigham Young, second prophet and president of the Mormon Church, *Journal of Discourses* 3:93	the most High." Isaiah 14:13–14. God's reply: "Yet thou shalt be brought down to hell." Isaiah 14:15
How many gods?	**How many gods?**
There are many gods. "How many gods there are, I do not know. But there never was a time when there were not gods." Brigham Young, *Journal of Discourses* 7:333	Only one God in Three Persons, Father, Son and Holy Spirit. "For there is one God, and one mediator between God and men, the man Christ Jesus." 1 Timothy 2:5 The Mormon view is polytheism — many gods. It is NOT Christianity.
Deity of the Lord Jesus	**Deity of the Lord Jesus**
The Mormon Jesus is not prayed to.	"My Lord and my God." John 20:28 "Let all the angels of God worship Him." Hebrews 1:6 The Lord Jesus is worshipped by men and angels, on earth and in heaven, and only God can be worshipped. Most cults deny the deity of the Lord Jesus Christ, but the Lord Jesus is not "a" god; He is **God,** Second Person of the Trinity.
Jesus' birth	**Jesus' birth**
Born in Jerusalem. *Book of Mormon, Alma* 7:10) This is a different Jesus. You cannot be born in two places.	Born in Bethlehem. Micah 5:2; Matthew 2:1

Mormonism says:	The Bible says:
Nature of Jesus	**Nature of Jesus**
Jesus is the "spirit brother" of Lucifer.	The Lord Jesus is the only begotten Son of God. John 3:16 & 18 "…God sent His only begotten Son into the world…" Since there is only one Son, He has no "spirit brother".
Salvation	**Salvation**
Joseph Smith decides who gets to Heaven. "No man or woman in this dispensation will ever enter into the celestial Kingdom of God without the consent of Joseph (Smith). . . " "He reigns there as supreme a being in his sphere, capacity, and calling, as God does in heaven." From *Journal of Discourses*" Vol. 7, p. 289. "No salvation without accepting Joseph Smith.." *Doctrines of Salvation* Vol. 1, p. 188.	"I (the Lord Jesus) am the way, the truth, and the life: no man cometh unto the Father, but by me." John 14:6 "…if thou shalt confess with thy mouth the Lord Jesus, and shalt believe in thine heart that God hath raised him from the dead, thou shalt be saved." Romans 10:9 Faith in Jesus Christ guarantees our salvation and Joseph Smith has no say in this.
Salvation is based on good works including baptism, missionary work, good deeds etc.	"By grace are ye saved through faith, and that not of yourselves: it is the gift of God, not of works, lest any man should boast." Ephesians 2:8, 9
"…for he that is tithed (pays 10 per cent of his income) shall not be burned…" *Doctrine & Covenants* 64:23	Money we give has nothing to do with our salvation. The reference to burning is just to put fear into people.
"Celestial marriage and a continuation of the family unit enable men to become gods." This is one of the headings for *Doctrine and Covenants* 132.	Salvation does not depend on our being married. Single people go to heaven too!

Mormonism says:	The Bible says:
Jesus in the USA?	**Jesus in the USA?**
Jesus came down and preached in the United States. *Book of Mormon 3* Nephi Chapters 11–18	The Lord Jesus preached throughout Israel, and He gave His disciples the job of taking the gospel throughout the world.
Wedding at Cana	**Wedding at Cana**
"Jesus was the bridegroom at the marriage of Cana…We say it was Jesus Christ who was married… whereby he could see his seed." Orson Hyde, Apostle, *Journal of Discourses*, Vol. 2, p. 82.	The Lord Jesus was one of many guests at the wedding in Cana. He had no earthly wife or children.
Polygamy — plural marriage	**Polygamy — plural marriage**
"…the Latter-day Saints have embraced the doctrine of a plurality of wives, as a part of their religious faith." *Journal of Discourses* Vol. 1:54, Orson Pratt, 1852

"…if any man espouse a virgin, and desire to espouse another… he cannot commit adultery for they are given unto him…" *Doctrine and Covenants* 132:61

"…and if he have ten virgins given unto him by this law, he cannot commit adultery, for they belong to him…" *Doctrine and Covenants* 132:62

Mormon Apostle George Q. Cannon declared, "If plural marriage be divine, as the Latter-day Saints say it is, no power on earth can suppress it, unless you crush and destroy the entire people." At the October General Conference Apostle Franklin D. Richards | Polygamy is a crime in America and was one reason why the Mormons were not welcome in any Christian community, and were driven out of various places. It may also be one reason why over 100 men stormed the Illinois jail where Smith was being held on a charge of treason and shot him dead.

Americans have always valued freedom of religion and it is in the Bill of Rights. American people did not "persecute" early Mormons for their faith, but for their criminal activity — polygamy. They were revolted by the activities of Mormon leaders and horrified by the numbers of people who were attracted to the Mormon faith.

Joseph Smith knew he would have trouble getting his wife Emma to |

'Take heed lest any man deceive you'

True or False?

Above: Jehovah's Witnesses HQ in New York. They say they believe the Bible, but JWs study it with their own brand of Bible teacher. They think we are in the Millennium reign of Christ already and believe only 144,000 people are going to Heaven; other believers are the 'great crowd' who will inherit the earth. All others will be annihilated in JW land. None of this is biblical, of course. Picture: ***Daniel Franklin***

Above: The Bahai Shrine of the Bab perched above Haifa Harbour in northern Israel. Bahai is an offshoot of Islam — Islam minus the violence.

Above: A huge Mormon temple in St. Louis, Missouri. Mormon temples are not open to the public. They are exclusive centers where secret ceremonies are carried out. Mormons can have their marriages "sealed" at the temple. This makes it a "celestial marriage" for eternity, even though the Lord Jesus said there was no marriage in Heaven. Mormon doctrine says that the man can then become a "god" with his own planet to populate with his children. Mormons also get their magic underwear in the secret temple rites (see Table of Truth : Mormons vs. the Bible).

Take a drive down Weidman Road in the affluent west county of St. Louis, Missouri, and you will see: an Islamic mosque (above) and a Hindu temple (below).

Jerusalem — 'a cup of trembling'

Above: Jerusalem, mentioned about 800 times in the Bible. God's special city, His chosen place on earth where the Lord Jesus Christ was crucified, buried and rose on the third day. The city where the Lord paid the penalty for our sins, and where He will return in glory. Picture: *Daniel Franklin*

Left: Alan in the studio of Genesis Television in London, with a backdrop of Jerusalem. You will find a *Jerusalem Post* news ticker on our website, *www.thefreepressonline.co.uk* and you can click on any of the stories to read the full reports.

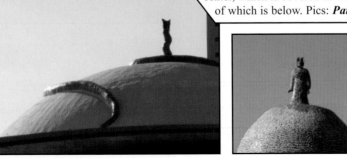

The hiss of the serpent in Israel... this loathesome sight is in Haifa, an otherwise beautiful city in Israel. The huge snake adorns the central dome of a new shopping center, which is covered in weird art, some of which is below. Pics: *Pat Franklin*

The beast is rising

The woman is riding the beast in this amazing sculpture. It is in the plaza of the town of Breisach, Germany, and commemorates the founding of the European Union. A plaque says the woman is the mythical Europa, but Rev. 17 also tells of the woman and the beast. Bible commentators identify the woman as symbolizing the end times one world Rome-based church and the beast as Antichrist's one world government. In verse 16 the beast turns on the woman and destroys her. This will happen because, while Antichrist will use the ecumenical Roman church to consolidate his power, he will want to be worshipped himself, and will not tolerate any other religion. Picture: *J. Taylor*

Judgement of the damned

Freemasons sometimes have a white throne on their graves. According to the Bible, the Great White Throne is the place of the judgement of the damned *(Rev 20)*, where degrees of punishment are determined. This judgement is at the end of the 1000 year millennial reign of Christ. Christians do not go through the Great White Throne judgement, but the Bema judgement seat of Christ, where rewards for service are handed out *(1 Cor 3: 12-15)*. The Masons believe they will stand before God at the Great White Throne, wearing their white aprons, showing their good lives, but the Bible teaches that all our good deeds are like filthy rags *(Isaiah 64:6)* and that none are righteous *(Romans 3:12)*. Only faith in Christ saves us. Our advice to Freemasons: Come out of the lodge while there is time!

'No god but Allah!' — writing in stone on a Freemasons' Shriners' Mosque in Missouri

Left: A Shriner told us the Arabic writing on the blue background on their shrine mosque in Springfield, Missouri, was "just decoration". We had it translated by Arab Christians in Israel. It says: "No god but Allah". The Shriner talking to us thought he was a Christian, but he was deceived. Shriners, if they want to be saved, must put their faith in Christ alone. And they must come out of that evil organization!

Evolution? It never happened!

There is a layer of grey sediment called the KT Boundary all over the earth. Below the layer are dinosaur bones. Above the layer: no dino bones. Why? Because the layer marks an "extinction event" – otherwise known as the Flood of Noah. Read the  amazing story of the KT Boundary on our website, *www.thefreepressonline.co.uk* Picture: *Georgina Walker*

Above left: The crumbly colored cliffs of Alum Bay, Isle of Wight, England. They are so delicate that you are not supposed to touch them, yet we are supposed to believe that they have been there for millions of years! No, just 4,500 years, since the time of Noah's Flood. **Above right:** Chunks of the colored chalky rocks which we found on the beach below the cliffs, with the marks they make.

The shop on the left is in Fleet High Street, Fleet, Hampshire, England. We noticed some stalactites growing where the porch roof overhangs the sidewalk. Inset is a close-up of one of the stalactites, about three inches long at the moment, but growing fast. Just another indicator that nature did not need millions of years to form the things we see.

A fine ammonite found by our daughter Annie on Charmouth beach in southern England. Like all fossils, this critter was perfectly formed, not in the process of evolving into anything. And it was suddenly buried in sediment in some catastrophe, namely the biblical Flood.

Right: Our beautiful blue planet pictured from the moon. And every so often, that lifeless ball of moon rock is precisely positioned in the exact right spot between us and the sun so that we get the fabulous sight of a solar eclipse, the sun totally blacked out and just a thin ring of fire hanging in the blackness. Statistically impossible that such a celestial event could ever happen, but it does. The Lord programmed it into the heavens. Truly awesome. Picture: *Nasa*

Get clued up!

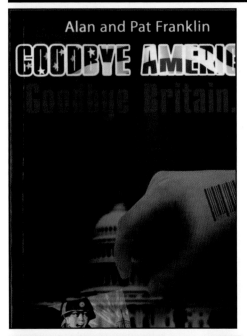

These are our first two books, the second of which, *Goodbye America, Goodbye Britain*, is selling out fast. This book sets the scene for the world financial crisis, predicting it from current events and Bible prophecy several years before it began. It looks at the underlying spiritual malaise which created the problems in our sin-sick societies and shows how nations' sovereignty is being subsumed into the coming New World Order – the end of the nation state. The Satanic one-world spiritual movement which accompanies it is also described. Packed with Biblical truth and wisdom from Scripture, this is a book like no other. Available while stocks last from *thefreepressonline.co.uk.*
The EU:Final World Empire book sold out its first two printings and we are set to rewrite, update and reissue its new edition in 2010, as we are always being asked for copies. Watch our website for news of this and the DVDs which are issued every year as Alan updates and expands his presentations.

Unlike most end times publications and presentations, Alan and Pat bring journalists'writing, researching and editing skills to all these products, making them easily understood and yet Biblically sound, which is why they sell so well with virtually no promotion.

As well as selling individual copies we sell bulk orders at discounts for eight or more books. Alan is available to speak to churches in America, Canada and Britain and is available via *thefreepressonline.co.uk.*
Our Christian ventures are non-profit-making.

Find out the facts!

Alan writes: These DVDS and our books are the main way we get vital information out to Christians. They are the product of hundreds of hours of reasearch by both of us and cover many topics seldom mentioned in most churches today — vital things like prophecy, the role of Israel, what happens next in the Middle East — and how the Bible never leaves us in ignorance. So add these teaching DVDs to your church library and open up those parts of the Bible that Satan has persuaded the church are "off limits." The EndTimes News double DVD is 4.5 hours teaching and the Prophetic Witness DVD is about two hours. See *thefreepressonline.co.uk.*

A great gift from Israel

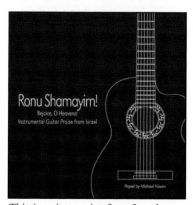

This is guitar praise from Israel, an instrumental CD 31 minutes long, by a gifted musician called Michael Nissim, who is also our son-in-law. It features classical guitar arrangements of modern Hebrew worship songs. The title means "Rejoice O Heavens" and it is available from the website of Michael and Annie Nissim, israelunique.com, linked to our website, *thefreepressonline.co.uk.*

One true God, many pretenders

Right: This cross delighted us as we drove across America. It must have cost someone a lot of money, but what a witness! One of the joys of travelling the interstate highways is the sight of crosses that people have put up to testify to the wonderful salvation won for us by the Lord Jesus on that terrible cross.

Pictures by Pat Franklin

Baal and Astarte idols found in Israel

Have you ever wondered what Baal looked like? Here he is (right), a rather silly looking thing. And below is Astarte, sometimes on her own, sometimes holding a baby. These broken bits of cheap pottery were actual "gods" worshipped by Israelites and dug up in recent years. These particular ones are at the museum at the little settlement of Dor, south of Haifa. For centuries the Jews were warned not to worship these useless objects, but they took no notice. Consequently, the Assyrians came down and flattened Israel in the north, selling the people into slavery. Then they attacked Judah in the south. The Assyrian army was destroyed by God outside Jerusalem *(see Isaiah Chapters 36 and 37)*, but Judah too was guilty of worshipping Baal, and it was left to the Babylonians to destroy Jerusalem and Solomon's beautiful Temple in 586 B.C. What a price Israel paid for their disobedience! And how like them we are today, worshipping false gods, following false prophets, believing false gospels, while ignoring the true God.

It is time to get your act together, folks! True or false? What and who are you putting your trust in? If your faith includes statues of Mary, Buddha, or any other object, it is time to get the sledgehammer out!

After seeing the Baal idols in Israel, we drove up the coast and happened to see these remarkably similar garden gnomes for sale. They even wear the same kind of hats as Baal! If you have such an item in your garden, you probably also have a hammer somewhere...

Mormonism says:	The Bible says:
declared, "...the government has determined that polygamy shall be abolished, but the government of heaven had previously determined that polygamy should be established..." *Journal of Discourses,* Vol. 20, pp. 276, 314	accept more wives, so he conveniently got a special "revelation" naming her and threatening her with death if she did not accept this teaching. (see below: "Special prophecy for Emma Smith")
Plural marriage is necessary for exaltation to godhood.	
Joseph Smith had many wives, some sources say about 30, some more. They included some teenagers and one girl reportedly aged 14; Brigham Young had up to 55 wives, and at one time threatened to throw them all out with their children if they did not stop whining.	
In the 1890s the LDS church dropped polygamy after the U.S. Congress threatened to seize all church lands, but they still have not removed the teaching from their "scriptures".	
Plural marriage is sometimes called an "ennobling and exalting principle" and sometimes referred to as "whoredom" depending on which Mormon teachings you read.	
Mormon women will be eternally pregnant in heaven, populating their husband's planet.	Count me out!
Special prophecy for Emma Smith (wife of Joseph Smith)	**Special prophecy for Emma Smith (wife of Joseph Smith)**
"And let mine handmaid, Emma	Bible is silent.

Mormonism says:	The Bible says:
Smith, **receive all those** (extra wives) that have been given unto my servant Joseph, (or she would be destroyed) saith the Lord God." *D&C* 132:52 "...then shall my servant Joseph do all things for her, even as he hath said; and I will bless him and multiply him and **give unto him an hundredfold** in this world, of fathers and mothers, brothers and sisters, houses and lands, **wives** and children..." *Doctrines and Covenants* 132:55	
Cooking	**Cooking**
Women "need to be taught, when their husbands bring into the house a hundred weight of flour, not to throw it out of the door..." "...and when they make bread of it, to make it light... instead of making cakes as indigestible as a whet-stone..." *Journal of Discourses* 10:28, Brigham Young, 1862. It sounds like his wives couldn't cook.	No cookery advice.
Expensive linen hankies	**Expensive linen hankies**
Brigham Young complained that some Mormon ladies insisted on only linen for their hankies, "applying them to their nasal protuberances with such refined grace ...and they want at least three dozen of them... then they wash them too often, wearing them out..." He said it was just too "...tiresome and expensive..."	Bible is silent on the subject of hankies.

Mormonism says:	**The Bible says:**
Brigham Young, 1862, *Journal of Discourses* 10:29	
Whining women	**Whining women**
"...my women... I want to do something to get rid of the whiners..." "...I will free every woman in this territory at the next conference..." "I will not hear any more of this whining." (The women had two weeks to decide if they would stop whining and stay with their husbands, or get out; if they left, they were to take the children with them.) Brigham Young, *Journal of Discourses* Vol. 4, pp. 55-57	Whining is not grounds for divorce.
Need for more babies — the celestial law	**Need for more babies — the celestial law**
"If my wife had borne me all the children that she ever would bare, the celestial law would teach me to take young women that would have children." Brigham Young, *Journal of Discourses* Vol. 4, p. 56 Babies were needed to provide bodies for "the noble spirits which are waiting for tabernacles..." Vol. 4, p. 56 "Sisters, do you wish to make yourselves happy? Then what is your duty? It is for you to bear children,..." Brigham Young, *Journal of Discourses*, Vol. 9, p. 37	No such thing as "the celestial law". They just made it up. There are no "noble spirits" floating around waiting for women to get pregnant so that they can have a baby's body to inhabit. This sounds like the horror film *Rosemary's Baby* — a film we do NOT recommend.
The Precious Blood of Christ	**The Precious Blood of Christ**
"Blood atonement" — Jesus' blood atoned for most sins, but	"...This is my blood of the new testament, which is shed for

Mormonism says:	The Bible says:
not all. Some sins (like leaving the Mormon church) have to be paid for with your own blood… *Doctrines of Salvation* Vol. 1, pp. 134–135, *Journal of Discours-es* Vol. 4, pp. 53–54, *Mormon Doctrine*, pp. 92–93. This teaching puts our blood on a level with the precious blood of the Lord Jesus, which paid for our sins (if we believe in Him, the true Jesus, not a counterfeit Jesus). Our blood pays for nothing.	many." Mark 14:24 "…and the blood of Jesus Christ his Son cleanseth us from all sin." 1 John 1:7 "In whom we have redemption through his blood, even the forgiveness of sins." Colossians 1:14 "Much more then, being now justified by his blood, we shall be saved from wrath through him." Romans 5:9 Jesus paid for **all** my sins — and yours if you believe in the real Jesus, not the Mormon 'half-brother-of-Satan' Jesus
Communion	**Communion**
Mormon communion is bread and water.	The Lord's Supper is bread and wine, representing Christ's body and His blood.
The angel Moroni	**The angel Moroni**
Joseph Smith claims he was visited several times by the angel Moroni[3], who directed him to gold plates hidden in the ground. The gold plates supposedly contained the material for the Book of Mormon.	"Beloved, believe not every spirit, but try the spirits whether they are of God: because many false prophets are gone out into the world." 1 John 4:1 "Though we, or an angel from heaven, preach any other gospel unto you than that which we have preached unto you, let him be accursed." Galatians 1:8
Prophets	**Prophets**
Joseph Smith claimed to be a	"Many false prophets shall rise,

[3] We know the names of only two of the good angels: Michael, who guards Israel, and Gabriel, the messenger who spoke to Mary about the birth of the Lord. Gabriel was also sent to tell Zacharias about the birth of John the Baptist. We know the name of only one of the fallen angels: Abaddon (Rev 9:11). "Moroni" does not make an appearance in the Bible and if he exists at all, he would be a fallen angel.

Mormonism says:	The Bible says:
prophet of God and Mormon leaders ever since have also claimed to be prophets.	and shall deceive many." Matthew 24:11 "Beware of false prophets, which come to you in sheep's clothing, but inwardly they are ravening wolves." Matthew 7:15 See some of Smith's false prophecies below.
Secrecy	**Secrecy**
"Temple Mormons" — the elite Mormons — take part in secret ceremonies in the temples. The temples are separate from the Mormon churches and are not open to the public. Most Mormons never attend the temple. They must have a "temple recommend" to be eligible and to get that they have to be scrutinised by a bishop, who will check to see if they have been paying the tithe.	"In secret have I said nothing." John 18:20 Jesus is the light of the world. Christian churches are open to all and there are no exclusive centers and no secret ceremonies. You can come along even if you never give one penny.
Oaths	**Oaths**
Temple Mormons take oaths.	"…I say unto you, swear not at all…let your communication be, yea, yea; nay, nay: for whatsoever is more than these cometh of evil." Matthew 5:33–37. No oaths.
Priests	**Priests**
Temple Mormons pray that the "power of the priesthood be upon me and my posterity forever."	"Ye also, as living stones, are built up a spiritual house, a holy priesthood…" 1 Peter 2:5 "But ye are a chosen generation, a royal priesthood, a holy nation…" 1Peter 2:9 "…Unto him that loved us… and hath made us kings and priests…" Revelation 1:5–6

Mormonism says:	The Bible says:
	Every believer in the Lord Jesus is a priest in that they can go direct to God the Father in prayer through faith in Christ.
Melchizedek priesthood	**Melchizedek priesthood**
"…and (they — believers) are priests of the Most High after the order of Melchizedek…" Many Mormon men claim to be priests of the order of Melchizedek (an Old Testament leader to whom Abraham gave 10 per cent of the spoils of war.)	Only Jesus Christ holds this title. See Hebrews Chapters 5-10. The Lord Jesus is the high priest who offered His own blood once for all. The early Christians were not urged to seek the "Melchizedek priesthood", as there was no such thing. Whoever claims to have this title now is usurping the role of Jesus Christ.
Symbols	**Symbols**
Mormons do not use the cross as a symbol, but they do use Masonic and satanic symbols like the upside down star, the all-seeing eye, the compass and square, sunstones and moonstones.	Christians do not need symbols of any sort.
Tithing your income	**Tithing your income**
Mormons are expected to tithe 10 per cent of their income to the church.	"Every man according as he purposeth in his heart, so let him give; not grudgingly, or of necessity: for God loveth a cheerful giver." 2 Corinthians 9:7 We do not have to tithe. That is Old Testament. We are not under the Mosaic Law, but under grace, and we are to give as we purpose in our hearts. This is part of our liberty in Christ. Anyway, the usual 10 percent sounds too little. If you've paid off your mortgage and the family is provided for,

Mormonism says:	The Bible says:
	why not help some poor people, sponsor a missionary etc? "He which soweth sparingly shall reap also sparingly; and he which soweth bountifully shall reap also bountifully. 2 Corinthians 9:6
Garden of Eden	**Garden of Eden**
The Garden of Eden was in Jackson County, Missouri.	I (Pat) am from Missouri, and the Garden of Eden it ain't — and never was! The location was in the Middle East, near the Tigris and Euphrates rivers. The Tigris and Euphrates rivers are nowhere near Missouri.
The Second Coming	**The Second Coming**
Jesus is coming back to Independence, Missouri.	"…why stand ye gazing up into heaven? This same Jesus, which is taken up from you into heaven, shall so come in like manner as ye have seen him go into heaven." Acts 1:11 His feet will stand on the Mount of Olives, which is not located in my home state.
Jesus' capital city	**Jesus' capital city**
Independence, Missouri, will be the new Jerusalem, the capital of the world in the Millennial reign of Christ. "…God will build up in Jackson County, Missouri… the New Jerusalem." *Journal of Discourses* Vol. 21, p. 314	Jerusalem, Israel, not Independence, Missouri, will be the capital of the earth and the Lord Jesus will reign from there. The New Jerusalem is quite a different thing — read about this wondrous place in the Book of Revelation Chapter 21.
Coffee	**Coffee**
Mormons do not drink coffee or tea.	"Not that which goes into the mouth defiles a man: but that

Mormonism says:	The Bible says:
	which comes out of the mouth, this defiles a man." Matthew 15:11 "...In the latter times some shall depart from the faith, giving heed to seducing spirits and doctrines of devils... commanding to abstain from meats (different foodstuffs)..." 1 Timothy 4:1-7. Forbidding certain foods is a "doctrine of devils."
Israel	**Israel**
"I do not wish to again hear any of the **leaders of Israel** complain that there is not any pure sugarcane seed, flaxseed, cotton seed etc..." Brigham Young *Journal of Discourses* 10:34, 1862	Israel is in the Middle East. It is not in Utah. Mormons are not Israelites.
Baptism of the dead	**Baptism of the dead**
Doctrine and Covenants (D&C) 128 sets out the Mormon doctrine of baptizing dead people, God's plan for "the salvation of the dead." (128:1–8) This goes against Smith's later teaching in *D&C* 131:6, which says: "It is impossible for a man to be saved in ignorance."	"...it is appointed unto men once to die, but after this the judgement." Hebrews 9:27 God is the righteous judge. He doesn't need us to go through a ritual for someone else. Everyone is judged for what they themselves believe and do. People who died before the time of Christ will be judged with perfect fairness. "Shall not the Judge of all the earth do right?" Genesis 18:25 All our chances of salvation end at death.
New revelation	**New revelation**
The Book of Mormon is new revelation from God.	"For I testify unto every man that hears the words of the prophecy of this book. If any man shall

Mormonism says:	The Bible says:
	add unto these things, God shall add unto him the plagues that are written in this book…" Book of Revelation 22:18 The canon of Scripture is closed. There is no new revelation. We have everything we need in the Bible.
Another gospel	**Another gospel**
The whole title of the Mormons' main book is "The Book of Mormon: **Another** Testament of Jesus Christ."	"I marvel that ye are so soon removed from him that called you into the grace of Christ unto **another gospel**: which… would pervert the gospel of Christ." Galatians 1:6, 7
Adding to the Bible	**Adding to the Bible**
The Mormons have four books of scripture, putting their own three above the Bible, which they say has been mis-translated. The Mormon scriptures are: *Book of Mormon, Pearl of Great Price, Doctrine and Covenants* and the Bible.	"If any man shall add unto these things (the scriptures in the Bible), God shall add unto him the plagues that are written in this book." Book of Revelation Chapter 22:18 You add to the Bible at your peril! They not only add to the Bible, but they put their own writings *above* the Bible!
Accuracy	**Accuracy**
Joseph Smith says the *Book of Mormon* "was the most correct of any book on earth and the keystone of our religion…" I have read it and I can think of no book containing as many inaccuracies as the *Book of Mormon*.	The Bible, unlike the *Book of Mormon*, has been verified countless times in various ways. We have the indisputable evidence of many fulfilled prophecies; a mountain of textual evidence; a huge body of archaeological evidence; historical evidence; and the evidence of 2,000 years of

Mormonism says:	The Bible says:
	changed lives, transformed by the power of the gospel.
Racism	**Racism**
"And the skins of the Lamanites were dark, according to the mark which was set upon their fathers, which was a curse upon them…" *Book of Mormon*, Alma 3:6 "Had I anything to do with the negro, I would confine them by strict law to their own species…" Joseph Smith, *History of the Church*, Vol. 5, pp. 218–219 The penalty for inter-racial marriage was "death on the spot — this will always be so." Brigham Young, *Journal of Discourses* Vol. 10, p.110 "…for the seed of Cain were black…" *Pearl of Great Price*, Moses 7:22 The LDS church reversed its racist position in 1978. This could have had nothing to do with the possibility of losing their tax exempt status.	We are all one race, descended from one man and one woman. There is no mark or curse on anyone.

The *Book of Mormon* has a sub-heading: "Another testimony of Jesus Christ". The introduction claims that it is "a volume of holy scripture comparable to the Bible … It is a record of God's dealings with the ancient inhabitants of the Americas… the most correct of any book on earth…"

Published by Joseph Smith in 1830, he claimed to get the information for the *Book of Mormon* on gold plates from an angel named Moroni. The *Book of Mormon* purports to be the history of a Jewish family who sailed to the Americas in about 600 B.C. The father was called Lehi. Nephi was the good son; Laman the bad son, and his descendents were cursed with a black skin. The *Book of Mormon* claims that this Jewish family peopled the continent, and their descendents are the American Indian tribes. It tells of people and kings, cities, battles, wars and nations for which there is no evidence whatsoever.

Mormon scientists have disproved the *Book of Mormon* by DNA testing of 150 Indian tribes. None of the Indians are descended from Jews. This fact alone marks out Joseph Smith as a false prophet. And it means that the "most correct book on earth" is provably, indisputably untrue, a work of fiction, a lie purporting to be the truth.

Mormon people today are known as god-fearing, hard-working, decent, moral people, and I suspect that most of them have never read the *Book of Mormon* for themselves. Nor have many of them examined the DNA evidence which reveals the truth about their religion. They are trying to live good lives and they hope to please God and go to heaven; and although they are sincere, they are sincerely wrong. They do not closely examine their beliefs, or hold their leaders to account. They follow a false prophet and believe a false gospel, which will not save them. The foundation of their religion is a lie, and the *Book of Mormon* is just a badly written work of fantasy, a fictional epic which has no basis in reality at all. It claims to be true history, but it is a fairy tale.

We gave the DNA evidence video to one Mormon family. They said: "If this is true, the *Book of Mormon* is false. We will write to the leaders in Salt Lake City and try to find an answer." They never did come back to us with an answer.

There is also the money question. The Bible indicates that where there are false prophets and false teachers, the sheep are going to get fleeced.

"...false prophets... false teachers... shall bring in damnable heresies... many shall follow their pernicious ways... and through covetousness shall they with feigned words make merchandise of you..."

2 Peter 2:1–3

In our Christian fellowship, giving is "as you purpose in your heart," not tithing a specific amount. No one knows how much anyone else gives, but we all know where every penny goes. The accounts are presented in detail at the annual meeting. Every church member is given a copy and we are encouraged to examine them and urged to publicly question the church leaders if we have any misgivings. No one is paid a salary at our church. No one personally benefits from the money that is given. From the very beginning of their religion, Mormons were under pressure to tithe at least 10 per cent of their income and their documents contain many instances of heavy pressure being applied.

However uncomfortable it may be, Mormons should begin to critically examine their religion. God gave us brains and expects us to use them. He is not displeased when we analyze, delve into scripture, look for solid answers. In fact that is exactly what He wants us to do! The truth can always stand up to a good, hard examination. But false prophets will hide behind a smokescreen. They do not want you to look too closely, and will discourage any close investigation.

God, on the other hand, says in the Bible:

"Come now, let us reason together"   Isaiah 1:18

"Gird up the loins of your mind!"   1 Peter 1:13

In other words — put your thinking cap on! Get clued up! God wants you to know the truth, because the truth will set you free.

Conclusions:

- **The Book of Mormon is not true.** DNA has disproved it.
- **There is no marriage in Heaven** according to the Lord Jesus Christ, the only One who really knows. Matthew 22:30; Mark 12:25. This knocks out the central teaching of Mormonism — that of celestial marriage.
- **Therefore — the Book of Mormon is not Christian.**
- The first two points above are enough on their own — Mormons should come out of their false church and find a good Bible believing Christian fellowship.
- The teaching that Mormon men can become gods is satanic!
- "Celestial marriage and a continuation of the family unit enable men to become gods." This is one of the headings for *Doctrine and Covenants* 132, which Mormon doctrine says is holy scripture, above the Bible. But their "celestial marriage salvation" is not salvation at all. It is pagan. It will not make them gods. It will take them to hell, not to heaven.

One thing I have noticed about false religions is that they use art to entice and entrap people. The beautiful pictures of attractive people are like a lure. There are several pictures like this in the *Book of Mormon.* Like the false tale of the Nephites and Lamanites, they are just fictional, and they are there to appeal to the eyes. We pray that the Lord will open the eyes of Mormons.

Another prop used so deceitfully in the *Book of Mormon* is the use of a phoney Elizabethan-style English to make it sound like the King James Bible. This is an attempt to give the *Book of Mormon* some kind of credibility. It also confuses the reader. Truth is mixed in with error. This is the case throughout LDS documents. Confronted with the documentary evidence of what their religion really teaches, many Mormons would probably say: "I don't believe that."

If any Mormon is reading this, we hope that you will rise to the challenge and put your religion under the microscope of your intellect. There are many websites you can go to, run by Christian discernment ministries and also by ex-Mormons who have seen the truth and left the LDS church. If you don't have internet, it is available at your local library; the librarian will help you.

A Christian friend who has had dealings with a Mormon said he suspects that the Mormon religion can cause people to develop a massive ego. My friend's comment was this: "I told the others about the Mormon belief that the men could become gods with their own planets, and they said, 'No wonder X has such a massive ego — he thinks he's going to be a god!'" That Mormon man believes the lie, the lie that Satan whispered to Eve in the Garden of Eden:

"Ye shall not surely die... ye shall be as gods..."

Genesis 3:4, 5

Are you believing the lie? Millions of Mormons believe it. But the Word of God, the Holy Bible, tells us the truth: "...before me there was no God formed, neither shall there be after me." Isaiah 43:10

Time to come out, dear people.

Some of the false prophecies of Joseph Smith, founder of the Mormon religion

- The Lord supposedly commanded a city called Zarahelma to be built in Iowa as a gathering place for the saints from all points on the compass. *Doctrines and Covenants* 125. This settlement was abandoned a few years later.
- "Judge ye for yourselves... I feel, like Paul, to glory in tribulation; for to this day has the God of my fathers delivered me out of them all, and will deliver me from henceforth; for behold, and lo, **I shall triumph over all my enemies**, for the Lord God hath spoken it." *Doctrines and Covenants* 127:2. Far from tri-

umphing over his enemies, two years later Joseph Smith died in a gun battle trying to escape from jail. He shot and killed two people and wounded a third, so he cannot by any stretch of the imagination be considered a martyr.

- He said that the Civil War in America would spread to all nations. It didn't. *Doctrines and Covenants* 83:5
- He said the slaves would rise in rebellion in the south. They did not. *Doctrines and Covenants* 87:5

Some of the silly things in Doctrines and Covenants

- How to tell if an angel is good or bad — shake hands with him and if you can feel his hand, he is a good one; if you cannot feel anything, he is a bad one. *Doctrine and Covenants* 129
- Joseph Smith claimed to be a descendent of Abraham. That would make him either a Jew or an Arab. *Doctrine and Covenants* 132:30
- Joseph Smith was no great shakes at writing, so he prophesied a PR man for himself in *Doctrines and Covenants* 124:12. "… verily I say unto you, let my servant Robert B. Thompson help you to write this proclamation…"
- Spring Hill, Missouri "is named by the Lord Adam-ondi-Ahman, because, said he, it is the place where Adam shall come to visit his people, or the Ancient of Days shall sit, as spoken of by Daniel the prophet." *Doctrine and Covenants* 116. No, Daniel did not refer to Missouri in his wonderful book.

Modern Mormons claim to be Christians. In our research we used **their own foundational books.** If they really **are** Christians, they will want to find out the truth of this matter.

Websites where you can read the Mormon foundational books for yourself online:

Book of Mormon and *Doctrines and Covenants* are at http://scriptures.lds.org/bm/contents.

Pearl of Great Price, a weird, garbled piece of writing which plagiarizes the Bible, can be read at www.sacred-texts.com. It contains the alleged history of Joseph Smith in which he sees a vision of God the Father pointing to His Son (Chapter 1:17 of the history). This alone would mark it as a false, for no one can see God the Father and live.

Journal of Discourses is at www.journalofdiscourses.org.

Chapter 9

Table of Truth:
Jehovah's Witnesses vs. the Bible

Started by: Charles Taze Russell in 1872.
Numbers: About 7 million.
Headquarters: Brooklyn, New York.
Publication: *The Watchtower* magazine.
False prophecies: Millennial reign of Christ started in 1873; Christ's return was in 1874; Armageddon in 1914; end of the world and kingdom of God established in 1915; reign of Christ to start in 1925; return of Abraham, Isaac and Jacob (a house in San Diego was purchased for them).

Jehovah's Witnesses say:	The Bible says:
Deity of Christ	**Deity of Christ**
Jesus Christ is not God. The JWs have their own paraphrase version of the Bible, *the New World Bible*. The JW's *New World version* states in John 1:1 that "the Word was with God and the Word (Jesus) was "a god".	"In the beginning was the Word, and the Word was with God, and **the Word was God**." John 1:1 Jesus is God. "…being in very nature God…" "For in Him dwelleth all the fullness of the Godhead bodily." Colossians 2:9 "My Lord and my God…" "Let all the angels of God worship Him (Jesus)." Only God is to be worshipped

Jehovah's Witnesses say:	The Bible says:
	according to the First Commandment: "I am the Lord thy God... Thou shalt have no other gods before Me." Exodus 20:2, 3

Therefore, since Jesus received worship and is to be worshipped, He is God. Like all the cults, JWs diminish the Lord Jesus in one way or another. They pull Him down from His rightful throne. |
| **Creator** | **Creator** |
| Jesus was created; He is not the Creator. | "For by Him were all things created, that are in heaven, and that are in earth, visible and invisible, whether they be thrones, or dominions, or principalities, or powers: all things were created by Him and for Him: and He is before all things, and by Him all things consist." Colossians 1:16, 17

The Lord Jesus is most definitely the Creator of all things. |
| **The Trinity** | **The Trinity** |
| No such thing as the Trinity. Only God the Father is God. | Three persons in one God. God is one, but He is a plural God. He calls Himself Elohim, which is a plural noun in Hebrew. In English it is translated as "us": "Let US (Elohim — plural) make man..." Genesis 1:26

"...baptizing them in the name of the Father and the Son and the Holy Ghost..." Matthew 28:19 |
| **The Holy Spirit** | **The Holy Spirit** |
| The Holy Spirit is not a person, just a spiritual force. | "Satan filled thine heart to lie to the Holy Ghost... thou hast not |

Jehovah's Witnesses say:	The Bible says:
	lied unto men, but unto God." Acts 5:3, 4
	"…baptizing them in the name of the Father and the Son and the Holy Spirit…" Matthew 28:19 The Holy Spirit IS a person, and IS God.
The Resurrection	**The Resurrection**
Christ was raised from the dead as a spirit person — not a physical person.	"Behold my hands and my feet, that it is I myself: handle me, and see, for a spirit hath not flesh and bones, as ye see me have." Luke 24: 39
Hell	**Hell**
The wicked will be eternally destroyed. No hell, no eternal conscious punishment. Annihilation.	"…the rich man also died, and was buried; and in hell he lifted up his eyes, being in torments…" Luke 16:22, 23 "To go into hell, into the fire that never shall be quenched: where their worm dieth not, and the fire is not quenched." Mark 9:43, 44 "Fear not them which kill the body, but are not able to kill the soul: but rather fear him which is able to destroy both soul and body in hell." Matthew 10:28
Heaven	**Heaven**
Only 144,000 people go to heaven. They are the "little flock" of Luke 12:32. Most other people are in the "great crowd" who will live on an earthly paradise. Those not worthy to be in the great crowd are annihilated.	The 144,000 are in Chapters 7 and 14 of the Book of Revelation — all are Jewish men, 12,000 out of each tribe. The tribes are even named, so this cannot be spiritualized to mean Jehovah's Witnesses. The 144,000 are all virgins and all know a special song

Jehovah's Witnesses say: **The Bible says:**

no one else can learn, and they go everywhere Jesus goes. This is a particular group of Jewish men in the end times, not the total of all people who get to heaven. Anyone claiming to belong to this elite group would have to be from one of the named tribes, be a virgin and know a song no one else can learn.

Also in Revelation Chapter 7 are the "great multitude which no man could number" seen in heaven and v 14 tells us they have all come out of the Great Tribulation. This is another particular group, the many people martyred in the Tribulation.

Then there is another multitude, possibly even greater — all those who have died or will die and go to be with the Lord, and also those of us who are alive and go up in the Rapture. All will be in heaven with the Lord. How do we know this? Because the Lord Jesus promised it: "He that believeth on Me hath everlasting life." John 6:47

"For God so loved the world, that He gave His only begotten Son, that **whosoever** believeth in Him should not perish, but have everlasting life." John 3:16 — and many other verses. Any number can be saved — **whosoever** comes to faith in Christ.

Jehovah's Witnesses say:	The Bible says:
The Cross	**The Cross**
The Lord Jesus did not die on a cross. JWs insist that He was impaled on a stake, a single piece of wood, with one nail through both hands.	Christianity has always taught the cross. There is also abundant archeological evidence of people crucified on crosses in that era. It was the Roman method of crucifixion for the condemned man to carry the crossbeam, which was fixed to the upright beam. Doubting Thomas said: "Unless I see in His hands the print of the **nails** (plural)…" John 20:25
The Name "Jehovah"	**The Name "Jehovah"**
The JWs believe that 'Jehovah" is the correct pronunciation of the name of God.	The Lord Jesus referred to God as "Father" over 100 times in the gospels. Believers are in a family relationship with our loving heavenly Father.
Works	**Works**
You should go door to door with copies of *The Watchtower* magazine and try to convert people.	"For by grace are ye saved through faith; and that not of yourselves: it is the gift of God: not of works, lest any man should boast." Ephesians 2:8, 9 Nothing we can do would ever contribute to our salvation. It is a pure gift of God to all those who trust in the Lord Jesus as their Savior.
Soul sleep	**Soul sleep**
The human soul ceases to exist at death. When you die as a believer, you go into an unconscious state until the resurrection.	Your body may die, but your soul is conscious and either goes straight to be with the Lord forever, or straight to hell. "…the beggar died, and was car-

Jehovah's Witnesses say:	The Bible says:
	ried by the angels into Abraham's bosom (the holding place for Old Testament saints until the Lord had redeemed them at Calvary)." Luke 16:22. (The beggar, Lazarus, is named, so this was a true story, not a parable.) "The rich man also died, and was buried: and in hell he lifted up his eyes…" Luke 16:22, 23 "…willing rather to be absent from the body, and to be present with the Lord." 2 Corinthians 5:8
When it all started	**When it all started**
JWs were begun in 1872 by Charles Taze Russell, who called the new religion the Watch Tower Society and began publishing a magazine by that name. He denied the deity of Christ and the Holy Spirit and promoted his own (mis)interpretations of the Bible. He based much of his teaching on measurements of the Great Pyramid at Giza, Egypt. His publishing business was virtually a guaranteed success since the adherents of the cult were expected to buy it or give donations for it. The name was changed to Jehovah's Witnesses when Joseph Rutherford took over the publishing business in 1916.	The church began on the feast of Pentecost when the Holy Spirit came upon the apostles and disciples in the upper room. Despite the worst that Satan and misguided men could do, the true church continues and will continue, because the Lord said: "…I will build my church and the gates of hell will not prevail against it." Matthew 16:18 Jesus' church is His people and, while it is unfortunate that we have so many denominations, His people are those who have been born again of the Holy Spirit — regardless of church affiliation.
Translators	**Translators**
The translators of the JW Bible, the New World version, were at first anonymous, but it is gener-	The original Hebrew and Greek texts of our Bible have been translated by learned men into Eng-

Jehovah's Witnesses say:	The Bible says:
ally believed that four men did the work, none of whom could read Hebrew or Greek. The New World "translation" was made to fit the theology of the JWs.	lish, starting with John Wycliffe in the 14th century. Wycliffe was an Oxford professor and scholar. William Tyndale (16th century), martyred for his translating and publishing, was a genius fluent in eight languages. They accepted the deity of Jesus Christ. Many other excellent translators followed, scholars who were experts in Hebrew and Greek.
Membership	**Membership**
Possibly seven million JWs worldwide.	All those whose names are written in the Lamb's Book of Life! Is your name written down in glory? If you do not accept the deity of Christ, your name will not be there.
Michael the Archangel	**Michael the Archangel**
Jesus was Michael the Archangel, but then he became a man. *The New World,* p. 284	Michael the Archangel is a formidable angel who would no doubt take great exception to the JWs' teaching about him, since one of his jobs is to watch over Israel, and he would be very careful never to claim the glory owed only to the King of Israel, the Lord Jesus Christ.
Blood transfusions	**Blood transfusions**
Blood transfusions were a sin, but now the leadership is wobbling on this. Witnesses have died rather than accept a blood transfusion and they thought they were pleasing God. If the leadership changes its stance on transfusions	Life-saving medical procedures are not forbidden in the Bible. The scriptures which the JWs use dealing with blood are not talking about medical procedures, but animal sacrifice and eating or drinking blood. A blood transfusion has

Jehovah's Witnesses say:	The Bible says:
now, there could be expensive litigation.	nothing to do with animal sacrifices and if you have one, you are not eating or drinking blood.
Communion	**Communion**
Only the 144,000 should take communion and no one is sure who they are. The JWs celebrate the Lord's Supper only once a year and hardly anyone partakes of the bread and wine — mostly those who believe themselves to be one of the 144,000. This is so sad and so very wrong.	"Take, eat; this is my body." Matthew 26:26. The Lord Jesus did not say only 144,000 could obey Him in this. 1 Cor 11:23–34. In those scriptures and others it is clear that every baptized believer may and should join in, in order to remember the Lord's death until He comes back. The Lord Jesus did not set a number. He invites ALL to come!

Some of the failed prophecies of the Jehovah Witnesses: 100% failure rate

- 1889 — Prophecy that the Battle of Armageddon would take place in 1914. "…the battle of the great day of God Almighty, Rev 16:14, which will end in 1914 A.D. with the complete overthrow of earth's present rulership…" from *Studies in the Scriptures,* Vol. 2, *The Time Is At Hand,* 1889 ed, p. 101.
- 1889 — Millennial reign of Christ began in 1873 — "… we shall by showing that it (the Millennium) began in 1873, be proving that we are already in it." *Studies in Scriptures*, Vol. 2, p. 40, 1889.
- 1889 — "Christ came in the character of a bridegroom in 1874…" *Watchtower*, Oct 1879, p. 4.
- 1897 — "Complete destruction of the powers that be of this present evil world… about the close of the Time of the Gentiles; October A.D. 1914." Charles Taze Russell, *Studies in the Scriptures*, IV, p. 622.
- 1897 — "Our Lord, the appointed King, is now present, since October 1874 A.D. and the formal inauguration of his kingly office dates from April 1878." *Studies in the Scriptures*, Vol. 4, p. 621.

- 1915 — "The present great war in Europe is the beginning of the Armageddon of the Scriptures Rev 19:16–20." Charles Taze Russell, *Pastor Russell's Sermons*, p. 676.
- 1915 — It was "an established truth that the final end of the kingdoms of this world, and the full establishment of the kingdom of God, will be accomplished near the end of 1915 A.D." *The Time is At Hand*, 1915 edition, p. 99.
- 1920 — Prediction of the physical return of Abraham, Isaac and Jacob in 1925. (*Millions Now Living Will Never Die*, published by Watchtower, 1920, pp. 89–90).
- 1922 — "The period must end in 1925... the climax is the fall of Satan's empire and the full establishment of the Messianic kingdom..." *Golden Age,* Jan 4, p. 217.
- 1922 — "What further evidence do we need? ...it is an easy matter to locate 1925..." *Watchtower*, May 15, p. 150.
- 1923 — "1925 is definitely settled by the Scriptures...the Christian has much more upon which to base his faith than Noah had..." *Watchtower*, April 1, p. 106.
- 1924 — "No doubt many boys and girls who read this book will live to see Abraham, Isaac, Jacob, Joseph, Daniel ..." *The Way To Paradise*, p. 226.
- 1924 — "The year 1925 is a date definitely and clearly marked in Scriptures..." *Watchtower* p. 211.
- 1925 — "The year 1925 is here. With great expectation Christians have looked forward to this year. Many have confidently expected that all members of the body of Christ will be changed to heavenly glory during this year. This may be accomplished. It may not be. Christians should not be so deeply concerned about what may transpire this year." *Watchtower,* Jan 1, p. 3.
- 1925 — "The difficulty was that the friends inflated their imaginations beyond reason..." *Watchtower* p. 56.
- 1926 — "Some anticipated that the work would end in 1925, but the Lord did not state so." *Watchtower,* p. 232.[1]
- 1930 — Large home purchased in San Diego for resurrected Old Testament saints like King David to live in, but the deeds made out for Joseph Rutherford. Rutherford (who had a drinking problem) took over from Russell.[2]

---

[1] References to JW false prophecies can be found at www.carm.org, bible.ca and many other websites.

[2] From *The Jehovah's Witnesses: Their Beliefs and Practices* by Doug Harris, Reachout Trust.

How the JWs almost scrambled my mind

When I (Pat) was a new Christian in 1981, two JWs came to our house. "Oh good, I thought, I will try to convert these poor, deluded people." Within a few minutes they had my head spinning as they went through their patter. They had been very well trained in what to say and how to say it, and they very nearly scrambled my brain as they attempted to convince me that Jesus was not God. As we went round and round, getting nowhere, I finally said: "Let's pray." The senior JW replied: "Oh, no, we can't pray with you; we wouldn't be praying to the same God." How right she was. Indeed we would not.

Time went by, and we were on vacation on the Isle of Wight when, once again, two JWs came to the door. I knew I had to get the matter settled once and for all. I asked them to come back later in the day, and when they had gone, I sat down with my Bible and started searching. I KNEW Jesus was God, but how to prove it to myself and to them? As I read through the scriptures, the Lord reminded me through them that He was worshipped, and He did not stop people worshipping Him. Also the angels worship Him. And I was reminded of the Ten Commandments, which forbid the worship of anyone or anything other than God Himself. Therefore, Jesus HAD to be God; there was no getting round it. I was so happy to get to this point, and by the time the JWs came back, I had my scriptures ready. Never again did any of them have a hope of shaking my faith in the deity of my Lord and Savior.

For more scriptural proof of the deity of Christ, read our chapter, "Things Every Christian Should Know". And do some research yourself. There are many more proofs that the Lord Jesus is, in fact, God.

Conclusion:

It is no small thing to diminish the Lord Jesus Christ. With its belittling of the Lord Jesus, its twisting of scripture, its flawed version of the Bible, and its many failed prophecies, we are absolutely appalled that any rational adult could still be a member of the Jehovah's Witnesses. We call on any of them who may read this chapter to leave this organization immediately! Turn instead to the true Jesus, the way, the truth and the life. Come to Him and He will set you free!

Chapter 10

The Seventh Day Adventist Cult

"Beloved, believe not every spirit, but try the spirits whether they are of God: because many false prophets are gone out into the world."

1 John 4:1

"And many false prophets shall rise, and shall deceive many."

Matthew 24:11

Adventists are a dangerous cult because most Christians have no idea they were founded on false prophecies, unbiblical ideas and the writings and visions of an uneducated woman who was a proven liar and plagiarist.

- Their number one doctrine is Saturday worship. Sunday worship sends you to hell. *(The Bible says we are saved by grace through faith and nothing more. Ephesians 2:8-9)*
- Few people know they teach vegetarianism.
- They say that Jesus is Michael the Archangel yet also believe that Jesus is God. Jesus is God, He is the Creator *(John 1:1–3; Colossians 1:16–17; Hebrews 1:1–6)*; whereas, Michael is just an angel, a created being. (Source*: several hundred SDA weblinks!)*
- Adventists believe in "soul sleep"; that all other churches are teaching Satan's lies and that they, the Seventh Day Adventists, the SDA, are the only true church. All cults and isms, from Catholicism onwards, teach that they are the one true church!
- Twice their founder predicted Christ's return and the end of the earth. When it didn't happen, they invented a new doctrine to

cover up the error. Christ had returned, but to heaven, to clean up the heavenly sanctuary. This, they say, He has been doing since 1844.

- Adventists think that the mark of the beast is Sunday worship and that in the Tribulation (the final seven years prior to Christ's return) the third angel of Revelation 14:9 will go forth to warn the world about Sunday worship. Ellen G. White, high priestess of Adventism, claimed to have been taken to heaven in a vision and shown a halo round the Sabbath commandment. Strange that the Lord Jesus never taught Saturday observance!

- Under "Fundamental belief 13," Adventists say they are the remnant church of the last days. "This remnant announces the arrival of the judgment hour, proclaims salvation through Christ, and heralds the approach of His second advent. This proclamation is symbolized by the three angels of Revelation 14; it coincides with the work of judgment..." (Source: *adventist.org*). The real remnant church comprises true born-again believers, not cults like Adventism. And we will not be here during the Great Tribulation — see our chapter on the Rapture.

- Adventists do not believe that the Bible's repeated clear references to the nation of Israel in end times prophecy mean what they say. Like most of today's major denominations and cults, they think the church has replaced Israel and now has the blessings God intended for His special nation on earth. The whole of the Bible relates to Israel and its past and future play a pivotal role in prophecy. A key scriptures is: "And I will bless them that bless thee, and curse him that curseth thee..." This is God's covenant with Abraham (see *Genesis Chapters 12, 15, 17 and 22),* a covenant confirmed with Isaac (Genesis 26) and Jacob (Genesis 28) and also with Joshua (Joshua 1:2, 4).

- This covenant was renewed with Isaac, but NOT Ishmael, so it is clearly the land of Israel and Jewish people that receive the everlasting blessing of God. Everlasting means just that. Any possible doubt is cleared up in Numbers 6:27: "And they shall put my name upon the children of Israel; and I will bless them." The prophets of old speak to us today, for those with ears to hear. Pat and I explain more of the end times scenario in our book, *Goodbye America, Goodbye Britain*, available from our website *thefreepressonline.co.uk.* Other DVDs and teaching materials are regularly added.

- The Adventists' interpretation of prophecy is symbolic or wildly distorted. Adventist websites like *pickle-publishing.com* sell books decrying the modern prophetic role of Israel — and the "amazing fact" is that one of their leading spokesmen, author Steve Wohlberg, is described as "a Jewish believer and Bible scholar." The blurb goes on: "Steve Wohlberg gets to the root of the problem, the role of Israel, in the excellent video/DVD series, *Israel in Prophecy*. He exposes the errors of *Left Behind's* theology in a way that you can understand." In fact Tim LaHaye's *Left Behind* series of books, although fiction, was basically biblically sound.

- The Adventists' best known personality, TV presenter, pastor and spokesman, Doug Batchelor, is, "amazingly," another Jewish Adventist leader. Promoting Wohlberg's book, *Exploding the Israel Deception*, Batchelor, Director of the *Amazing Facts* Radio and Television Ministry, writes: "As a Jewish Christian, I am deeply concerned about the widely accepted distortions regarding modern Israel and Prophecy. . ." They do not believe that much of Bible prophecy is literal.

- They still look to Ellen White's teaching and their website states: "One of the gifts of the Holy Spirit is prophecy. This gift is an identifying mark of the remnant church and was manifested in the ministry of Ellen G. White. As the Lord's messenger, her writings are a continuing and authoritative source of truth…"

- Adventists believe that the atonement for sin through Jesus is not complete until He comes again; only your past sins are forgiven by grace up to that point. (*The Bible says that the atoning work of Jesus is finished, never again to be repeated. John 19:30; Hebrews 9:24–28.*)

- The SDA church believes in the annihilation of evil-doers, who they say will cease to exist after the final judgment. This doctrine is similar to that of the Jehovah's Witnesses, who were formed around the same time. (*The Bible says those who have rejected Christ will be cast into the Lake of Fire. Revelation 20:12–15.*)

- They believe we will have to stand in the presence of God to be judged without a mediator. (*The Bible says that there is one mediator between God and man, and that is the Lord Jesus. I Timothy 2:5.*)

- They believe that: "because our bodies are the temples of the Holy Spirit... we are to abstain from the unclean foods identified in the Scriptures." *(their own website: www.adventist.org)* The Bible says: "There is nothing from without a man that entering him can defile him: but the things which come out of him, those are they that defile the man." *Mark 7:15–20*
- They say humans are an indivisible unity of body, mind and spirit. They do not possess an immortal soul. *(source: Wikipedia)*
- They believe in something called the Investigative Judgment *(Fundamental belief 24, SDA church)* — a judgment of professed Christians which they say began in 1844, the year in which they predicted Christ would return to earth. In this judgment the books of record are examined for all the universe to see. The investigative judgment will affirm who is worthy of salvation, and vindicate God as just in His dealings with mankind. God, on the other hand, states in the Bible: "There is therefore now no condemnation to them which are in Christ Jesus..." *Romans 8:1*
- They believe that "increasing family closeness is one of the earmarks of the final gospel message." *(their website)*. The Lord Jesus said the exact opposite. "Now the brother shall betray the brother to death, and the father the son, and children shall rise up against their parents, and shall cause them to be put to death." *(Signs of the end times, Mark 13:12)*
- The SDA church often fails to make its identity clear and when a Christian we know was put on their mailing list and encouraged to distribute a video about "The Final Events of Bible Prophecy," he was told that as he went door to door trying to get neighbors to watch the video, he was to answer the question "what church are you with?" with this statement: "I am representing Amazing Facts, a Christian ministry that provides Bible study resources for people of all different faiths. My goal is to encourage others to read the Bible and learn how to find God." The facts about the SDA are indeed "amazing."
- When the SDA does one of its prophecy seminars they do it in style, with superb color brochures and leaflets and Powerpoint presentations, usually in a neutral location like a hotel. But their identity is not revealed until the end of various nights of talks and free gifts. Then the great secret comes out: you get the mark of the beast if you worship on Sunday!

Their main television show — and they are extremely media savvy — is called *Amazing Facts*, presented by Doug Batchelor, a top communicator who is also the pastor of Sacramento Central SDA Church, California. Doug is a convincing man and much of what he says is good. However, as Pat and I know Bible prophecy, we would watch aghast as Doug veered from good Bible teaching off to some surreal sideshow. Adventists have a garbled version of end times in which their church has a pivotal role. It does not.

The Hope Channel, the church's official TV network, features eight international channels broadcasting 24 hours a day on cable and satellite networks. The Hope Channel is also on three internet channels. Live satellite evangelistic events are aired by evangelists such as Batchelor, Mark Finley and Dwight Nelson, addressing audiences in up to 40 languages simultaneously. *(Wikipedia)*. There are private Adventist media outlets including the 3ABN and SafeTV networks. *Amazing Facts* and *The Quiet Hour* are on both radio and television and *Amazing Facts* is on the internet.

There are indeed some "Amazing Facts" behind the slick presentations, radio, TV and book ministries of the SDA, most of them not having the church name in their title, which should tell you a lot. They are so amazing we will now bring them into the light of day and see how they stack up against Scripture.

Sent to hell for worshipping on the "wrong" day? We don't think so! THIS is the day that the Lord has made, let us rejoice and be glad in it! This day, any day and every day. The early church met on Sundays, the first day of the week, Jesus rose on a Sunday and the birth of the church at Pentecost was on a Sunday (details in *Leviticus 23*, re the Feast of Weeks).

- The Lord Jesus appeared to His disciples on Sunday, the first day of the week *(John 20:19)*.
- Jesus appeared to eleven disciples on a Sunday, eight days after the first day of the week and meaning Sunday in the Jewish way of measuring days *(John 20:26)*.
- Peter preached his first sermon on a Sunday *(Acts 2:14)*.
- Three thousand new converts were baptized on the first day of the week- Sunday *(Acts 2:41)*.
- Paul spoke to Christians on the first day of the week *(Acts 20:7)*.
- Even the Revelation of the Lord to John was on the first day of the week *(1 Cor 16:2)*.

According to the claims of Seventh Day Adventist prophetess Ellen White, this would mean that those of us who attend church services on Sundays would join the early church and the disciples of the Lord in Hell. In her book *The Great Controversy Between Christ and Satan*, published in 1888, White stated (p. 605) that Sabbath worship, on a Saturday not a Sunday, would be the end times test that would separate those who were saved and those who would receive the mark of the beast. Revelation 13:16, 17 tells us that the mark of the beast is in fact a mark on people's right hands or fore-heads by which those on earth during the Tribulation period will signify allegiance to Antichrist. It has nothing to do with the day on which we worship.

- Ellen White, effectively the founder of Seventh Day Advent-ism, was a false prophet. In 1846 she had a vision, saying Ju-piter has four moons. It has 62 (Source, *NASA*) She claimed Saturn had 8 moons (correct number is 33) and Uranus has 6 moons (real number 27).
- Mrs. White taught that the Pope changed the Sabbath day and that Sunday observance was "the mark of the beast." While assorted popes have been guilty of much, this was not one of their failings.
- Ellen White taught for 65 years that the fall of Babylon applied to the protestant churches. In 1911 she switched and said it was the Roman Catholic Church.
- She said there was no more salvation for sinners after October 22, 1844 (the date when the Lord was supposed to have re-turned to earth).
- She predicted the American Civil War would end with slavery not abolished, the Union would not be preserved, the United States would be divided and England would intervene and de-clare war on America. Of course, the exact opposite happened.
- She forbade eating meat and wrote against eating butter and eggs. "Can we possibly have confidence in ministers who, at ta-bles where flesh is served, join with others in eating it?" *(Lake Union Herald, October 4, 1911).*
- In private Ellen White ate meat most of her life.
- She was a plagiarist and one of her books had to be suppressed because of this, and another revised. Even her main work, *The Great Controversy*, was in part lifted from elsewhere, uncred-ited.

- Adventists appear "evangelical" and most Christians think they are some form of protestant denomination. However, they believe they are the one true church, as they had a "true prophet" in their ranks, Ellen G. White. Privately they consider themselves to be spiritually superior to all other churches, and websites run by ex SDAs repeatedly confirm this. Their public image, polished by professionals, is not the whole story. You have to dig deeper.

Dudley Marvin Canright (1840-1919) was a man associated with Ellen White, going back almost to the Adventists' beginning, and kept all her early writings, some of the most damaging of which have been suppressed, he says. He once believed she was inspired by God, which she claimed to be. He states in his book, *Life of Mrs E. G. White, Seventh Day Adventist Prophet. Her False Claims Refuted:* "Every line she wrote.....she claimed was dictated to her by the Holy Ghost and hence must be infallible. Her people accept and defend these claims strongly. Her writings are read in their churches, taught in their schools and preached by their ministers the same as the Holy Scriptures. Their church stands or falls with her claims. This they freely admit. She stands related to her people (Adventists) the same as Mohammed to the Mohammedans, Joseph Smith to the Mormons, Ann Lee to the Shakers and Mrs Eddy to the Christian Scientists."

Mr. Canright's informative book, published in 1919, has been reprinted and is available today from Grant Shurtliff, Publisher, Sterling Press, Salt Lake City, Utah, U.S.A. Copies can be obtained from Grant at 910 West Montague, Salt Lake City, Utah, 84104 U.S.A. and we recommend it.

The observance of special days, as demanded by the Seventh Day Adventist cult, is denounced by Paul as legalism *(Galatians 4:10)*. The Council of Jerusalem did not command gentile converts to observe the Sabbath *(Acts 15:28, 29.)* It is made ever clearer in *Colossians (2:16, 17)* when Paul says that no man should judge you "in respect of any holy day, or of the new moon, or of the Sabbath days: which are a shadow of the things to come; but the body is of Christ."

We should have a day each week set aside for rest and worship, but it need not be Saturday, Sunday or any other day, although in practice most Christian churches meet on Sundays. When we visit Israel we happily attend services on Saturday — Shabbat — because that is how the born-again Christians there do things. (The nominal Christians meet on Sundays). We have no quarrel with this — but it has no relevance to our salvation. There is not one special day that we set aside for holiness. We are made new in Christ, old things have passed away. The Seventh Day Adventists are among today's Galatians as they want works — observances — to be added to God's grace before we can be saved. This is not a Christian concept.

The Adventists started wrong, predicted the end of the world on two separate wrong dates and should then have faded into well deserved obscurity, had it not been for a teenage girl — Ellen Harmon, later Ellen White — with visions. When aged nine Ellen was hit in the head by a stone which broke her nose and disfigured her for life. She was expected to die, but after being unconscious for three weeks, she came round, but avoided company and said: "My nervous system was prostrated." That was virtually the end of school for her and instead she became ultra religious and even hysterical, and then became a follower of William Miller, the honest but deluded man who turned into a prophet — a false prophet, a prophet of the Lord's return between March 21, 1843, and March 21, 1844. Ellen became engrossed in these predictions and attended meetings where people would fall to the floor, rather as they do in some off-beam churches today.

Some power was afoot, but it wasn't from God. "There was… the wildest fanaticism-dreams, trances, visions, speaking with tongues, claims of prophetic gifts and the like" (Canright, see above). Ellen Harmon, then 17, started having her own visions in December 1844, two months after "The Great Disappointment" of October that year, when Miller's revised date for the Lord's return, October 22, 1844, passed with nothing to report.

Beware of biblically ignorant people with visions: they often found false religions. That's how the Mormons started, with Joseph Smith's visions and subsequent false teaching. Mohammed got his false religion from an angel — a fallen angel. They all also believe they are the sole repositories of truth, the only true church and so on. For example, the Adventist phrase "coming into the truth" means believing and living the full SDA message and lifestyle (Source: *www.watchman.org*). The Adventist church was named in 1860 and formally incorporated in 1863 with 3,500 members in 125 congregations *(Encyclopedia of American Religion, Vol. 2, p. 681).*

Like many cults today, Adventists masquerade as conventional Christians and most Christians are in ignorance of their odd ideas. For instance, few Christians know that, following Ellen White's teaching, but not example, "about 50 per cent of Adventists today are lacto-ovo vegetarians" (Source: *International Vegetarian Union,ivu.org*). I became interested in them when a church we occasionally attended in the American Midwest hired an Adventist building while their own church structure was being built. The Christians met on Sundays when, of course, the Adventist building was empty. Adventist literature was all around and, as someone of spiritual inquisitiveness, I started to read. I was shocked to see the numbers: Adventists are gaining adherents more than three times faster than Mormons, which surprises most people. This is a church with a purpose, stated in *Adventist Today (www.atoday.com)*.

Under the heading: "The Ethos of Adventism" as: 1. Self-identity and Mission, Raymond Cottrell writes: "We Seventh Day Adventists like to think of ourselves collectively as the divinely appointed human agency through which the angel of Revelation 14:6-7 proclaims 'the everlasting gospel... to them that dwell on the earth, and to every nation and tribe and tongue and people' in view of the fact that 'the hour of [God's] judgment has come.' This angel implements the final phase of Jesus' commission to His disciples to 'go to all nations' and to witness for Him 'to the ends of the earth.' This sense of divine mission is the basic motivating factor in everything Seventh Day Adventist."

The official website of the Seventh Day Adventist Church says they are active in 201 countries. They claim a growth rate of around a million a year, with a new member joining every 35 seconds, and say the church doubles in size every 12 years. This is unsurprising considering the effort they make with "Sabbath Schools" — they are certainly not "Sunday Schools"! They claim 19,162,863 attend these schools — more than their total church membership of 15,660,347 *(December 2007 figure from church records)*. Wikipedia states their current membership to be over 17 million. Adventists also run 7,442 schools with nearly one and a half million children enrolled. There are high concentrations of Adventists in Central and South America, Africa, the Philippines and many other areas. Some 39 percent of Adventists are African, 30 percent Hispanic, 14 percent East Asian, and 11 percent Caucasian. In the United States they operate the largest Protestant educational system, second in size only to that of the Roman Catholic Church.

The facts on church growth among the cults are revealing. Here's a story from the heart of Mormon-land, Salt Lake City, Utah. *The Salt lake Tribune* reported (06/22/2006). Headline: *Keeping members a challenge for LDS churc*h. The LDS refers to the "Latter Day Saints," which is how Mormons describe themselves. The story runs "Mormon myth: The belief that the church is the fastest-growing faith in the world doesn't hold up... The claim that Mormonism is the fastest-growing faith in the world has been repeated so routinely by sociologists, anthropologists, journalists and proud Latter-day Saints as to be perceived as unassailable fact.

"The trouble is, it isn't true. Today, The Church of Jesus Christ of Latter Day Saints has more than 12 million members on its rolls, more than doubling its numbers in the past quarter-century. But since 1990, other faiths — Seventh Day Adventists, Assemblies of God and Pentecostal groups — have grown much faster and in more places around the globe. And most telling, the number of Latter Day Saints who are considered active churchgoers is only about a third of the total, or 4 million in the pews every Sunday, researchers say.

"For a church with such a large, dedicated missionary corps constantly seeking to spread its word, conversion numbers in recent years tell an unexpected story. According to LDS-published statistics, the annual number of LDS converts declined from a high of 321,385 in 1996 to 241,239 in 2004. In the 1990s, the church's growth rate went from 5 percent a year to 3 percent. By comparison, the Seventh Day Adventist Church reports it has added more than 900,000 adult converts each year since 2000 (an average growth of about 5 percent), bringing the total membership bringing the total membership to 14,300,000 (2006 figure)."

The Salt Lake paper adds: "When the Graduate Center of the City University of New York conducted an American Religious Identification Survey in 2001, it discovered that about the same number of people said they had joined the LDS Church as said they had left it. The CUNY survey reported the church's net growth was 0 per cent. By contrast, the study showed both Jehovah's Witnesses and Seventh Day Adventists with an increase of 11 per cent." Websites run by ex Mormons also doubt their world-wide numbers to be more than four million active members, since those who leave are still counted as members. They are being eclipsed by other cults, like JWs and Adventists, the latter in particular attracting many converts around the world, where the church has over 201,000 active employees. This is getting results: in Britain the Adventists have many young members among immigrant communities. A church with such active youth work and a young membership is clearly a future force.

Their past is even more interesting, founded as it is in error and humiliation.

It started with licensed, but not ordained, Baptist preacher and prophecy enthusiast William Miller, who believed that Daniel 8:14 showed that Jesus would return to earth in the year starting March 21, 1843. When March 21, 1844, passed without incident, the Millerites — for Miller had attracted a large following — were baffled. Miller did a recalculation and came up with the second date of October 22, 1844. What does the Bible say about false prophets? *Deuteronomy 18:22:* "When a prophet speaketh in the name of the Lord, if the thing follow not, nor come to pass, that is the thing which the Lord has not spoken, but the prophet hath spoken it presumptuously: thou shalt not be afraid of him." Adventism is a church built on a false prophecy, added to by a false prophetess.

You would assume that Miller's muddled ideas on prophecy and the failed date fiasco would have been the end of Adventism, but you would be wrong. Although this episode of two failed prophecies was called "The Great Disappointment," a hardcore group of Miller's followers continued to insist that the date was right. One of them, Hiram Edson, said he had a vision of Jesus at the altar in Heaven and his conclusion was that the Lord's return at the time had not been to earth, but to the heavenly sanctuary. So in 1844 Christ entered the Holy of Holies in heaven to begin His "Investigative Judgment." A Millerite called Joseph Bates picked up on this idea, putting out pamphlets, one of which was read and believed by Ellen G. Harmon, later to become Ellen White — the high priestess of Adventism. White never held an official church title, but became its acknowledged spiritual leader, claiming to have "the spirit of prophecy." *Adventist Today, The Ethos of Adventism,* states: "Ellen White identified herself as the messenger of the Lord to the church today."

Adventists believe "The Investigative Judgement" has been taking place in the heavenly sanctuary since 1844 — a doctrine clearly dreamed up to get early Adventists off the "false prophet" hook. Here D. M. Canright took up the story. Canright once believed Ellen White was inspired, as she claimed to be, in the same way as prophets of old. Every line she wrote- and she wrote many times more pages than are in the Bible — she claimed to have been dictated to her by the Holy Spirit, making her works infallible. Her key vision, in April, 1847, was of The Ten Commandments, with a halo of light round the fourth commandment. She deduced that this made it the most important — hence the Adventists' doctrine. She and her husband James, who was an Adventist preacher, had earlier read a tract about the Sabbath and had started to worship on Saturdays.

Here is Ellen White's source in her own words: "I am presenting to you that which the Lord has presented to me. I do not write one article in the paper expressing merely my own ideas. They are what God has opened before me in vision- the precious rays of light shining from the throne" *(Ellen G. White, Selected Messages, p. 27)*. The SDA Church printed this statement in their *Ministry* magazine in October 1981: "We believe the revelation and inspiration of **both the Bible and Ellen White's writings to be of equal quality.** The superintendence of the Holy Spirit was just as careful and thorough in one case as in the other."

White's "inspired" writings are read in the 64,017 Adventist churches, taught in their schools and preached by their 15,916 ministers as if they were Holy Writ.

The interesting thing about Ellen White is that she only had a third grade education and said for years she was unable to read. However, she not only read, but plagiarized other authors throughout most of her writings, which various researchers have established beyond doubt (for example, Walter Rea, *The White lie;* and *Judged by The Gospel)*. White called herself a "messenger" and claimed to have the spirit of prophecy and that her messages came from God to guide the church. Some followers called her "The Spirit of Prophecy," a blasphemous title. Today's Adventists admit that White cribbed from other authors.

Here again is *Adventist Today, The Ethos of Adventism*: "Where would the church be — or would it be — without Ellen White? The church has always acknowledged and appreciated the prophetic guidance of Ellen White, but her exercise of that gift has confronted it with a number of perplexing questions. Chief among these have been: her rather extensive use of the literary labors of others while claiming that everything she wrote came to her directly from heaven; the role of her secretarial assistants; and her pastoral use of Bible passages out of context.

"First to arise was the question of literary dependence. How could Ellen White's claim of divine origin for everything she wrote be reconciled with the fact that some of it was borrowed from other writers without giving them credit? For instance: Sixty-three passages consisting of approximately 15.4 percent of her *Sketches From the Life of Paul* (1883 predecessor of her 1911 *Acts of the Apostles*) were either direct, close, or a loose paraphrase of Conybeare and Howson's *Life and Epistles of St. Paul* (1852) and Farrar's *Life and Work of St. Paul* (1879).

"Three years later extensive passages in her *Manuscript 24*, 1886, were quoted almost verbatim from Calvin E. Stowe's 1867 *Origin and History of the Books of the Bible.*

"In 1888 the first edition of *The Great Controversy Between Christ and Satan* quoted at length from a number of historians such as Sir Walter Scott, James Wylie, and J. H. Merle D'Aubigne, again without giving credit. In 1970 and 1971 William S. Peterson, and in 1974 Don R. McAdams, documented her reliance on Protestant historians for material incorporated into it, including some of their historical errors." That's it, in an Adventist's own words (he goes on to give lots more detail.)

Vegetarians regard Ellen White as a great leader and example, and today the SDAs run natural food stores and vegetarian restaurants. Here's one of Ellen White's quotes from 1903: "Vegetables, fruits and grains should compose our diet. Not an ounce of flesh meat should enter our stomachs. The eating of flesh is unnatural. We are to return to God's original purpose in the creation of man." Well, it is true that in the Garden of Eden vegetarianism was the rule. It will also be the case in the Millennium that animals will cease to eat each other. However, following Noah's Flood, things changed when the Lord told Noah:

"Every moving thing that liveth shall be meat for you: even as the green herb have I given you all things."

Genesis 9:3

The Bible tells us:

"Beware of false prophets"   Matthew 7:15

Through the ages false prophets have arisen to mislead millions, even billions in the case of Catholics and Islamics. False churches like the Adventists share with other cults and isms the belief that their followers are the true saints and all other creeds and churches are apostate.

All false creeds also add to the Bible, with their own "sacred writings." The Adventists state in the third article of their creed: "That the Holy Scriptures of the Old and New Testaments were given by inspiration of God, contain a full revelation of His will to man and are the only infallible rule of faith and practice." Sounds good — but it's not so. Canright, who knew them well before he left, says Adventists believe that Ellen White's works are also given by inspiration from God, that these writings contain a fuller revelation of God's will to man, and that they are infallible. He adds that Mrs White repeatedly claimed her writings were inspired and placed them on a level with the Bible.

So it is odd that Adventists say that Jesus, the author and finisher of our faith, is none other than Michael the Archangel, and that the dead go into something called "soul sleep". Soul sleep is the idea that between death and resurrection the individual is effectively existing only in the memory of God. Adventists also believe that our sins will ultimately be borne by Satan, which makes the work of the Cross redundant and is a blasphemy. Our Lord said on the cross "It is finished." Our debt was paid in full and we were saved by His blood — NOTHING else, certainly not Sabbath observance. The failed date setting of October 22, 1844, has been transformed in Adventist theology into the date Jesus entered the second and last phase of His atoning work.

Remember, deception is the spirit of the age and is what the Lord Jesus expressly warned about in Matthew 24. I am sure there are many true Christians in the ranks of the Adventists. However, they are misled and mis-taught and should come out of this false church, this deceitful cult. God's attributes are truth and light *(1 John 1:5–6)*, whereas, Satan's qualities are darkness and lying *(John 8:44)*.

Chapter 11

Spiritism, Channeling, Psychic Fairs
by Alan Franklin

"Believe not every spirit, but test the spirits, whether they be of God. "

1 John 4:1

"Life goes on," says a sign on our local spiritualist (sic) church. Indeed it does. Unfortunately for the spiritists — the Bible's term for dabblers in the occult — it does not go on very well for them once they are "beyond the veil," as they like to put it.

Although I attended a spiritualist church as a young man and became a member of the Spiritualists' National Union in Great Britain, the world's largest organisation for spiritualists, according to its website, spiritualism seemed on the way out. Something for little old ladies trying to contact their dear departed.

But those of us hoping that this anti-Christian practice would die a natural death — with no contact hereafter — were too optimistic. I moved on to become a magazine writer and was recruited by a New Age organisation which, I was amazed to learn, was really spiritualism in a new form. They didn't use this term, though. They were "healers" and business people, aiming to usher in the Age of Aquarius. But they didn't take a business decision without contacting the "friends". The friends were spoken to at séances, just like the old-style spiritualists held. When Satan has a good con trick going, he won't let it go in a hurry. Why try new tricks when the old ones work so well? So spiritualism is not only still with us, it is stronger than ever, with psychic channels on television in which you can "call the psychic" on a minute-by-minute charge basis. Lucrative and popular.

I realised this when I borrowed some ladies' magazines to research an article. I was amazed to see many pages of classified ads offering tarot readings and occult consultations of all forms. Whole new generations have discovered that there is a spiritual world out there, something they can, perhaps, tap into. Except that the Bible expressly forbids this. Leviticus 19:31: "Regard not them that have familiar spirits, neither seek after wizards, to be defiled by them." Leviticus 20:27: "A man or a woman that hath a familiar spirit, or that is a wizard, shall surely be put to death." In Isaiah 8:19 there is another warning about practising spiritism, the seeking after "familiar spirits," today called spirit guides. Odd that in the spiritualist churches I attended they never read those passages out.

Of course, today's psychics usually don't bother with church: they are often busy touring the country with travelling psychic fairs, which pull in the punters at town halls near you. This is in the long tradition of occultism as a stage show. The Fox sisters founded modern spiritualism on March 31, 1848. This was the day Kate and Margaret Fox, of Hydesville, New York, claimed to have contacted the spirit of a murdered peddler. The alleged spirit communicated through rapping tables, sounds which onlookers heard. Thus started a whole tradition of rapping, tapping and ouija board consultation. The Fox sisters became the showbiz sensations of their time.

As a young reporter I sometimes rustled up a "spooky story" to sell to the more lurid tabloids. This is how I made my living and the cases were often convincing. Something was going on...so in the days of the Fox girls the papers splashed the story and soon the girls' alleged "communications with the dead" became a stage act eventually managed by PT Barnum of Barnum and Bailey's Circus fame. The Fox family were the world's top mediums and modern spiritualism was launched.

Unfortunately for the credibility of spiritualism, however, Margaret Fox later confessed that the whole thing was a hoax and the knocks were produced by, among other things, the cracking of her toes! She added that the Hydesville events were a pre-April Fools' joke prank which was taken too seriously! Her confessions were reprinted in *A Skeptic's Handbook To Parapsychology* by Paul Kurtz, 1985, Prometheus Books. However, she later withdrew her statements and tried to resume her career as a medium. It didn't work and the Fox sisters are said to have died as penniless drunks. There is always a price to pay if you allow Satan to use you, even if it seems like a joke, or just fun.

Here's another confession. Once, Pat and I held a table-top seance and asked for business advice. "Invest more," was the message. We did.

It was disastrous. Pat and I once interviewed a medium who went into a trance and spoke with the voice of a "male doctor." A deceiving spirit whose advice you would have taken at your peril. When I worked full time for New Age publishers/channelers, the business advice we got from the "friends" was invariably catastrophic. The publishing business eventually went broke. The man in charge, a self-appointed guru and all round nutcase, but a convincing nutcase, heard one day that he should turn his (very large) back garden into a golf course. He immediately hired a digger and set to work. The last time I saw it, it looked like a World War One battlefield. I could go on, but you get the picture. Even though you may give the credit to Satan and embrace his ways, he will always do you down and make you look a fool. And you will be a fool if you get into the occult in any way. As the Lord Himself said: "By their fruits ye shall know them."

The fruits of it were always disastrous, from broken marriages to sick people, ostensibly "healed" only to get some far worse disease. You see, Satan hates mankind and wants to destroy God's highest creation. He wants to make monkeys out of us and the occult is one way of doing that, by deceiving people that they are speaking to " Tibetan Masters," in the case of the man I worked for, or even just ordinary, but dead, old "Uncle Joe". Uncle demon more like. You may be amused to know that, quite by chance, the large limo that my boss drove around in, often with me — his "old son"— at his side, had the number plate 666. Yes, we called him "The Beast," but he put on a good show with his purple cloak and saintly pose, even taking healing services in Anglican churches. They were strictly showbiz. Thank God we got out of all that in the 1970s.

The showbiz theme moved smoothly into the modern era in the 1980s when actress Shirley MacLaine became a devotee of "channeling," the modern name for spiritism... Her spiritual journey was recounted in her book *Out on a Limb* (1983). But Shirley went out on a broken limb... She believes in reincarnation and her website invites you to take part in a survey on it.

Channelers/spiritualists have a wide variety of beliefs and many that I knew believed in reincarnation, which is also the common belief of spiritists in South America. Other spiritists/New Agers told me they were in touch with Venusians! They were certainly in touch with something... but the Bible says there is no such thing as reincarnation. Hebrews 9:27 says that it is appointed for men to die once. Resurrection is the hope Paul presents for the dead in 1 Corinthians 15, not reincarnation. The point is, resurrection predicates a belief in one life, one death and a final judgment. There are no second, third or fourth chances.

Channeling and the search for "spirit guides" is now featuring on TV science fiction shows. On Star Trek's Voyager the First Officer is an American Indian named Chakotay. In an episode titled "The Cloud" he led Captain Kate Janeway in a meditation to enable her to get her own "animal spirit guide" (2/13/95). Cartoons and many other TV shows are often riddled with the occult in many forms. Truth and fiction are mixed as entertainment and people increasingly cannot tell the difference.

One who should have known the difference was Sir Arthur Conan Doyle, writer of Sherlock Holmes. Arthur is now one of the Spiritualist National Union's "honorary presidents-in spirit." After becoming the best known spokesman for spiritualism, Conan Doyle summed up its anti-Christian philosophy in his book *"The New Revelation"*, page 55: "One can see no justice in a vicarious atonement, nor in the God who could be placated by such means." So a leading spiritualist rejected the blood atonement which is the whole basis of Christianity — Christ's vicarious suffering on the cross for our sins. In no spiritualist church that I ever attended did a "spirit", speaking through a medium, ever say: "Jesus is Lord." For He was NOT their Lord. The Lord cast demons — "spirits" — out of people, He did not consult with them. There are many examples in the New Testament. Having disarmed principalities and powers, the Lord Jesus made a public spectacle of them, triumphing over them in it (i.e. "the cross" — Col 2:15). Perhaps this is why the spirits at psychic event do not like to talk about Jesus…

The rejection of the Lord's blood atonement continues in modern spiritualism. This quote from one spiritist church website *(Broad Street Spiritualist Church, Long Eaton, Notts, England)* sets out: "Personal Responsibility: This is the major doctrinal difference between spiritualism and orthodox religions. The basis of the Christian religion rests on the belief that Jesus died on a cross to save us from our sins. This we most strongly repudiate. Jesus was put to death by crucifixion for political reasons. This was the normal method of execution for most offences — including robbery. The Jewish priests were afraid He would usurp their power through his teaching and healing and the Romans that he might raise a rebellion against them — 'He stirreth up the people.'

"Spiritualism asserts that no one can save us from our wrong doing but ourselves. Man through his conscience knows the difference between right and wrong and is given free will to choose which road he will take. No one, be he religious or an atheist, can escape the consequences of his own mistakes. God does not sit in judgment over us, we have to be our own judges.

"What the church calls sin we regard as the violation of the divine natural laws made by God, which Paul interpreted when he wrote 'Whatsoever a man soweth that shall he also reap.' Man alone has to atone for his sins and not shirk his responsibilities."

The reader can make up his own mind what to think of churches which usually have crosses on or in their buildings and yet which dismiss the main basis of the Christian faith. If you love the Lord you obey His commandments, you do not call yourself a "Christian spiritualist", doing the exact opposite of what the Lord requires and which the Bible clearly sets out. The Seven Principles of Spiritualism are: 1) The Fatherhood of God; 2) The Brotherhood of Man; 3) The Communion of Spirit and the Ministry of Angels; 4) Continuous Existence of the human soul; 5) Personal Responsibility; 6) Compensation and Retribution Hereafter for all the good and evil deeds done on earth; 7) Eternal Progress Open to Every Human Soul.

So there is no sin, no judgement; we judge ourselves (how wonderful — I think most people would find themselves innocent!), we commune with demons although the Bible forbids this; we have the chance of "eternal progress" even though the Bible clearly states that we die once and then comes the judgement. The TRUTH is that we will never be saved by doing "good deeds" or taking "personal responsibility" but only by putting our faith and trust in the Lord Jesus, who shed His blood for us, died and on the third day rose again, giving us the chance of eternal life and forgiveness of sins. Remember, just one sin condemns us, and all have sinned. And as the spiritists don't seem to understand what sin is, let me explain. It is the breaking of the law, the transgression from God's law, 1 John 3:4. We are born with a sinful nature. Romans 3:23 says "all have sinned and come short of His glory." As for doing good, "There is none that does good, no not one." Romans 3:12. And Psalm 9:17 says: "The wicked shall be turned into hell..."

"My little children, these things write I unto you, that ye sin not. And if any man sin, we have an advocate with the Father, Jesus Christ the righteous: And he is the propitiation for our sins: and not for ours only, but also for the sins of the whole world. And hereby we do know that we know him, if we keep his commandments."

1 John 2:1–3

So if you claim to be Christian, you can certainly not be a spiritist, and born-again believers never would be, of course. But plenty of "nominal" Christians, even those who should know better, attend psychic meetings. One leading spiritist I knew well had formerly been a Baptist lay preacher, as the lure of "contacting the spirits" draws in millions.

If a rational thinker and doctor like Conan Doyle could fall for spiritist nonsense, there is some excuse for the ill-informed who flock to patronise the alleged psychics who "channel" on television channels. That's why we have written this book; so everyone can be well-informed. Writer Andrew Lycett wrote of Conan Doyle: "His support for spiritualism lent credence to some of the more outrageous frauds perpetrated on people desperately trying to get in touch with loved ones lost in the First World War. In his desire to prove the existence of spirits, he notoriously promoted two Yorkshire girls who, for a lark, claimed they had photographed the Cottingley Fairies (another proven hoax).

"After holding séances with his wife Jean to get in touch with members of their family killed in the first world war, Conan Doyle came out as a spiritualist. He claimed to converse with the spirits of the dead. Virtually abandoning Sherlock Holmes, Conan Doyle churned out books on spiritualism and addressed vast audiences around the world on the subject. He proudly adopted the sobriquet the 'St. Paul of the New Dispensation', ruffling some feathers along the way. In North America he clashed with Harry Houdini, an illusionist, who argued that all spiritualists' 'tricks' could be replicated by a competent magician." *Andrew Lycett's "Conan Doyle: The Man Who Created Sherlock Holmes," published by Weidenfeld & Nicolson in Britain and by Free Press in America.*

Writing about the mixed-up souls who seek out psychics is difficult, as they believe a multitude of fallacies. Here's what *Psychic News*, a paper I once subscribed to, reported in May, 1948: "How can we give the same message when half of us accept reincarnation and the other half hotly deny its possibility; when we have Christian spiritualists, Jewish spiritualists, Buddhist spiritualists and even… atheist spiritualists."

Remember, God's word, The Bible, forbids any attempt to get in touch with the dead. 1 Timothy 4:1-2 states: In the latter days some shall… give heed to seducing spirits and doctrines of demons." These are fallen angels, the angels who fell with Lucifer. We learn from Luke 16:26 that the dead cannot communicate with the living and those who have died in the Lord are forbidden from doing so. As for sorcerers

"They shall have their part in the lake of fire which is the second death." Revelation 21:8. Sorcery, witchcraft, all occult dabbling are the most serious of sins and a direct affront to God. This is why nations like the Canaanites were destroyed.

Spiritism — the Bible's term for spiritualism — opens people up to at the very least, silly deception, and at the worse, the possibility of demonic possession. Consulting or watching mediums is not harmless fun or showbiz. It is an offence to God and should be avoided at all costs — or the cost may be your eternal soul.

Chapter 12

Table of Truth:
Word of Faith vs. the Bible

Founder: No one person, but the main propagator in recent times was Kenneth Hagin. His followers carry it on, some of them big name ministries on religious TV.
Numbers: Unknown, but enormous.
Main book: The Bible, but with scriptures taken out of context and twisted.

Word of Faith says:	The Bible says:
God	**God**
God is bound to do your will if you do and say the right things.	God is sovereign. He acts in accordance with His holy nature, and He will honor His promises, but He is not to be manipulated by us. We cannot force Him to do anything. His ways are higher than ours and He sees the whole picture, the consequences and end of everything. Paul prayed three times for the thorn to be removed from his flesh, but the Lord's reply was: "My grace is sufficient." There was a reason for Paul's problem, and it was for his own good that he was suffering, hard

Word of Faith says:	The Bible says:
	as it seemed at the time. But, as he pointed out in Romans 8:18, "the sufferings of this present time are not worthy to be compared with the glory which shall be revealed in us." Paul's suffering glorified God.
Faith	**Faith**
Faith is a force. You can get what you want by positive confession.	Our faith leads to our trusting in the Lord, even in hard times — not using our faith to try to force God to act on our behalf.
Little gods	**Little gods**
Christians are "little gods"; Jesus is no longer the "only begotten Son" (because we are too); just as Jesus was "I am", we are "I am" too.	"Ye shall be as gods." Genesis 3:5. This is Satan's lie in the Garden of Eden; it is totally blasphemous, as these "little gods" will learn when they stand before the judgement seat of Jesus Christ.
Prosperity	**Prosperity**
God wants you to be materially prosperous, eating the best food, driving the best cars etc. Some Word of Faith teachers misconstrue the scripture from 3 John v. 2: "…I wish… that thou mayest prosper and be in health, even as thy soul prospereth." Also that Christ became poor so we could be rich.	Paul knew prosperity and knew poverty at different times. He did not consider it his right as a Christian to be well off. "Even unto this present hour we (apostles) both hunger, and thirst, and are naked, and are buffeted, and have no certain dwelling place…" 1 Corinthians 4:11 Paul was also scathing about the Corinthians, thinking of themselves as kings. 1 Corinthians 4:8 "Take heed, and beware of covetousness: for a man's life consisteth not in the abundance of the things which he possesseth."

Word of Faith says:	**The Bible says:**
	Luke 12:15 "And having food and raiment let us be content." 1 Timothy 6:8 "The love of money is the root of all evil…" 1 Timothy 6:10
Sickness	**Sickness**
It is your right to be healthy. You will be healed if you have enough faith.	"Trophimus have I left at Miletus sick." 2 Tim 4:20. Sometimes we do not get healed — nothing to do with our faith in Christ.
Mercy on the sick	**Mercy on the sick**
If you don't get healed, it's your own fault. You don't have enough faith.	"I was sick and ye visited me." Matthew 25:36 We are to visit the sick, not make them feel worse for not getting healed!
Money	**Money**
Give to get. Give more and you will get more. And the giving is to, guess who, the Word-Faith preachers, of course!	Give as you purpose in your heart. 1 Corinthians 16:2 Give to the poor, not to rich TV preachers or your local version of them.
Prayer	**Prayer**
Take authority in the name of Jesus and command things to happen. Bind the things that are bad. Loose the good things. To pray "Thy will be done" is feeble. You just take command.	In His darkest hour the Savior's prayer was: "Thy will be done," and He put it in the Lord's prayer, our model for how we should pray. Luke 11:2, Matt 26:39, Mark 14:36 Binding and loosing has to do with church government, not prayer. We cannot bind Satan. Paul did not bind evil spirits over the towns where he preached. Satan will not be bound until the end of the Great Tribulation, when a

Word of Faith says:	The Bible says:
	mighty angel with a chain will cast him into the Abyss, where he will remain until the 1,000 years are up. Revelation 20:1–3
Satan	**Satan**
Satan is under your feet. You bind him and remind him that he is under your feet and you are in charge.	"…these filthy dreamers… speak evil of dignities. Yet Michael the archangel, when contending with the devil … durst not bring against him a railing accusation, but said, The Lord rebuke thee. But these speak evil of those things which they know not…" Jude vs 8– 10 "And the God of peace shall bruise Satan under your feet shortly." Romans 16:20. God does this, not us! "…your feet shod with the preparation of the gospel of peace…" Ephesians 6:15. Our feet should be employed in taking the gospel to people.
The Lord Jesus	**The Lord Jesus**
Jesus was tortured three days and nights in hell. (This blasphemous teaching denies the atonement at Calvary.)	When the Lord Jesus died, he descended into Sheol, the underworld, which has four compartments: 1. Abraham's bosom, where the righteous people who died before the time of Christ were waiting for the Messiah to redeem them. 2. Hades or hell, the place of burning containing the souls of the damned. 3. The Abyss, where Satan will be bound for 1,000 years during the Millennium reign of Christ.

Word of Faith says:	**The Bible says:**
	4. Tartarus, the place of confinement for fallen angels who partnered with human women as mentioned in Genesis Chapter 6. 2 Peter 2:4, Jude v. 6
	When the Lord Jesus descended into Sheol, the underworld, he went to the section known as Abraham's bosom to preach to the spirits of Old Testament saints. There must have been the most incredible rejoicing ever down there! (Eph 4:8, 9)
	Then He led them to heaven (leading captivity captive), and gave them gifts — wow, we wonder what He gave them! Their bodies will rise later to be reunited with their spirits. Jesus did not go to the compartment known as Hades or hell, the place of the damned, separated from Abraham's Bosom by a vast gulf. There would have been no point in preaching to the damned.
	The Savior was NOT tortured in hell. His suffering had all been at Calvary.
Born again	**Born again**
The Lord Jesus was born again in hell and there defeated Satan.	The Lord Jesus is God. He never needed at any time to be born again. It is we, sinners all, who must be born again spiritually (John Chapter 3) because before that happens, we are dead in trespasses and sins. He did not defeat Satan in hell, but at the cross. Sa-

Word of Faith says:	**The Bible says:**
	tan was not then, and is not at the time of writing, in hell. He is going about seeking whom he may devour. Though Satan is a defeated foe, and Christ is king, our glorious King has not yet taken His earthly throne.
Dominion	**Dominion**
We can take dominion. We can transform the world because we have the dominion of earth.	"…all that will live godly in Christ Jesus shall suffer persecution. But evil men and seducers shall wax worse and worse, deceiving, and being deceived." 2 Tim 3:12, 13 We are never going to transform this world; it will only get worse. The Lord Jesus will transform everything when He returns; what we **can** do is to be obedient to the Great Commission and tell people about Him. Matthew 28:19
You can speak things into existence	**You can speak things into existence**
You can speak to your wallet and tell it to be filled with money; you can speak to your body and command it to be healed… etc.	This is occult. In Satanic pagan religions the witch doctor speaks out the things he wants to happen.
Visualize the things you want	**Visualize the things you want**
God can't answer your prayer unless you visualize the things you are trying to get Him to give you. For example, if you want a car, tell Him the make and color that you want.	Visualization is an occult technique. We never have to tell the Lord specifics. Matthew 6:25–34 teaches us that our Father knows everything we need and that when we seek first the kingdom of God, all these things will be given to us.

Word of Faith says:	The Bible says:
Seed faith	**Seed faith**
Sow some money into a rich preacher's ministry and you will get a lot more back.	Rubbish! Why would the Lord want you to give to these Word of Faith phonies who twist and abuse His holy Word?
Curses	**Curses**
At least one of the Word Faith teachers is on record speaking curses on critics and also on their children.	Proverbs 26:2 teaches us that an undeserved curse will NOT rest on the person it is aimed at. "Neither have I suffered my mouth to sin by wishing a curse to his soul." Job 31:30. Anyone who utters curses like this is sinning! It makes me shudder to think of someone who professes to be a Christian actually *cursing* another Christian. It reminds me of the bad prophet, Balaam, taking money to curse Israel, but the Lord turned it into a blessing (Nehemiah 13:2). So do not be afraid of any false teachers or any evil curses. Their curses cannot hurt you. God knows how to deal with such people. Vengeance is His. He will repay.

As new Christians in the 1980s we soon came under the influence of Word of Faith false teachers. We would like a refund, please, of all the money we foolishly sent to these wolves in sheep's clothing. We were gullible sheep and we got fleeced.

In the years (!) we were snared in all that, we learned virtually nothing about the Bible, although the preachers were constantly waving it around. We really thank the Lord for getting us out of all that and directing us to the great teachers who teach the Bible from a solid scholarly basis. We have learned so much from them; that is how we can write a book like this.

The man who first opened our eyes at that time (and has continued to do so!) was Dave Hunt. We were living in Britain, with no Christian radio to keep us informed, but we got Dave's The Berean Call newsletter every month, and he thoroughly exposed the false teachers and their false doctrines. It was a highlight of the month when the newsletter arrived. It still comes out each month, consistently brilliant and full of truth. You can read it online at *www.tbc.org* or subscribe and have it sent to your home. We cannot recommend this too highly.

Chapter 13

Global Non-Warming
and the Big Green Lie Machine
by Alan Franklin

"Concerning the weather, there is no way to win with the global Warming ideologues. If it is exceptionally cold, it is due to GW. If it is exceptionally warm, it is due to GW. If it is exceptionally dry, it is due to GW. If it is exceptionally wet, it is due to GW. If it is windy, it is due to GW. If it is calm, it is due to GW. It is ideological rather than scientific — just like evolution."

Dr. David Reagan, host of Lamb and Lion Ministries
and presenter of Christ in Prophecy

Global warming enthusiasts brook no contradiction. Ignoring all the "inconvenient truths" that refute their claims, they suppress scientific views that challenge them and howl "heresy" if ever a TV program circumvents the censors and tries to challenge their nonsense. For it is a faith being challenged — a false faith: green fundamentalism.

The global warming theory in a nutshell is this: the earth is warming up as a result of a build-up of carbon dioxide gas in the atmosphere, caused by people, and that the warming will increase catastrophically, endangering life on earth — and that hence, we must cut carbon emissions. More than 31,400 scientists around the world, over 9,000 of them Phds, have signed a document saying that this is not true.[1] The United Nations, on the other hand, believes in global warming to the uttermost, and claims there is a "scientific consensus" on it.

---

[1] See www.petitionproject.org.

I remember, back in the 1980s, watching TV films with graphics showing London under many feet of ice, with the towers of the Houses of Parliament peeking out over ice floes on the Thames. The scare then — also untrue — was "the coming ice age." On November 23, 1992, *Newsweek* magazine in the USA announced: "The advent of a new ice age, scientists say, appears to be guaranteed" and "the devastation will be astonishing." The claptrap certainly is. In less than ten years the tune changed to the world becoming a vast, hot desert. The media and the establishment, scientific and political, were emphatic about the prospect of a new ice age, as they are now about the prospect of the temperature rising. Any scare will do, it seems, and most people take it all as fact. Of course, Britain did have a little ice age in the 17th century, with dire effects on food production. Climate does change and it's warmer now, but this was unlikely to have been caused by 4 x 4 ox carts.

Then there was the other big scare of our time, the Millennium Bug. The computers would all fail as 1999 turned into 2000, we were told, because they had mostly been programmed with only two digits for the year instead of four. So, as the millennium dawned, computers would turn from '99 to '00 and think that it was 1900, which would give them all a nervous breakdown and shut down the world. As a newspaper editor at the time, I was deluged with official propaganda saying all this, some of which I have kept as evidence! The internet was awash with predictions that power stations would fail, water companies would grind to a halt, the lights would go out all over the world, computers would electronically die, airplanes could fall out of the air, and even car engines would not run.

Of course we know that none of this ever happened, and few of the prophets of doom ever apologized for this misleading claptrap. Some corporations totally changed their computer systems — just in case. The cost ran into billions, who knows how much? Some people stockpiled candles, canned and dried food, and even water in plastic bottles. Their cats were eating the tuna fish for years afterwards!

I made a point of publishing a newspaper opinion column the night before the new millennium, saying, relax — nothing bad will happen tomorrow. Pat and I walked home after midnight, in the early hours of the year 2000, and saw with some delight that the lights were on and planes were still flying. My career was safe!

As for global warming, I find it amazing that big media never seems to question it, and if the occasional global warming sceptic gets on air, they are attacked as if they are heretics. If you challenge perceived wisdom, life is often made uncomfortable. After Britain's Channel Four TV network screened *"The Great Global Warming Swindle"*, the new inquisition swung into action. There were 265 complaints to broadcasting watchdog OFCOM, whining that a "range of views" was not presented. The program was not criticized for the most part, however. Now I await (in vain) the "fair and balanced" reply to Al Gore's pseudo-scientific rants, which have been screened in many schools as if they were factual. Meanwhile, here are a few facts.

- So far in this century there has been no recorded global warming.
- All accepted measures of worldwide temperatures show the trend has been down since 2002. The world is getting colder! Meanwhile CO2 levels have been rising.
- The pre-eminent sea level scientist in the world says sea levels are NOT rising and has written a book about it: "The Greatest Lie Ever Told". (see end of this chapter)
- One single tide gauge in Hong Kong harbor showing a 2.3 mm rise was used to swing global sea level statistics and make it look as if there was a worldwide trend.
- Venice is not disappearing under rising sea levels. It is sinking, and should never have been built there in the first place.
- 31,000 scientists shattered the myth of "scientific consensus" on global warming. They signed a petition organized in 2008 by the Oregon Institute of Science and Medicine. Looking at consequences of increased carbon dioxide in the air they concluded: "Increases during the 20th century have produced no deleterious effects upon global weather, climate or temperature." Neither did they think they ever would, they added. And their petition states that there is substantial evidence that more carbon dioxide in the atmosphere produces "many beneficial effects"!
- The claim of a 0.5 degree °C temperature increase since 1980 is not confirmed by satellites or balloon measurements and may result from land based measuring near urban "heat islands". Or then again, maybe the reporting is just not honest.
- Solar activity (sunspots etc) has a close correlation with weather on the earth, but since we cannot do anything about the sun, and politicians cannot blame us for causing sunspots, this must be discounted.

- Solar magnetic flux shows trends similar to that for temperatures from 1880 to the present. The trouble with solar flares etc is that you can't slap a tax on them, as you can on carbon emissions.

- Temperature changes precede CO_2 changes. Al Gore's model makes it look just the opposite. An inconvenient fact. We await his apology for misleading the world.

- Christopher Monckton, a policy advisor to Margaret Thatcher, points out that in medieval times temperatures were as much as 5 degrees Fahrenheit warmer than now and Vikings farmed in Greenland, now a vast, frozen waste. The world then was obviously a warmer, pleasanter place, with much more room for food production. Global warming would be very good for farmers.

- Chinese sailed through the Arctic Ocean in 1421 and found no ice.

- "Every year since 1998 world temperatures have been getting colder, and in 2003 arctic ice actually increased. Why do we not hear about that?" — Prof David Bellamy.

- Ice in the arctic is often twice as thick as expected. Scientists from all over Europe returned from never-before-measured regions of the North Pole and *Euroreferendum Blog* reported on May 6, 2009 that instead of finding newly formed ice two metres thick, as they were expecting, they found it was double the thickness, up to four metres..

Polar bears are not endangered, despite all the pictures of them looking pathetic on small blocks of ice. In fact, their numbers are increasing rapidly due to hunting restrictions.[2] Ice in the Antarctic is above its 30 year average. Ice in the Arctic is close to its 30 year average. (source *Cryosphere Today* website and "Why Antarctic ice is growing despite global warming," *New Scientist* headline, 20 April 2009)

- Scary scenarios of the future are based on computer model predictions rather than real science. The computer models are only as good as the information fed into them.

- Carbon dioxide is what plants eat. The more of it there is, the better they grow. Let's pump out more and get bigger crops!

---

[2] www.sciencedaily.com. May 10, 2008. Also see our website www.thefreepressonline.co.uk and key in "global non-warming" for dozens of reports.

- President Obama's Energy Secretary Stephen Chu told a gathering of hand wringers at Prince Charles' St. James Palace in London (2009) that if all buildings and pavements were painted white the sun's rays would be reflected back into space and we'd all cool down a lot. Buy shares in paint firms is our advice (just joking).

The greenies know that their beliefs cannot stand close scrutiny. Heck, those handouts might stop rolling in. There are some big bucks to be had from governments for putting out scare research on non-existent global warming. The greenies were especially severe when respected environmentalist Professor David Bellamy, formerly one of the best known presenters on British television, questioned man-made climate change. I haven't seen him much of him on TV since then.

The *Daily Express* (London) published a revealing interview with Prof. Bellamy on Nov 5, 2008, headed: "BBC Shunned me for Denying Climate Change." Bellamy, a botanist and author of 35 books, presented around 400 programs. Then one day he committed an unforgivable crime: he stated that he did not believe in man-made global warming. He said: "The sad fact is that since I said this, I've not been allowed to make a TV program.

"I am a scientist and I have to follow the directions of science, but when I see the truth being covered up, I have to voice my opinions. According to official data, in every year since 1998 world temperatures have been getting colder, and in 2003 arctic ice actually increased. Why then, do we not hear about that?"

The reason, David, is that it's you who are out in the cold. Comments like this could be one reason: "At the beginning of the year there was a BBC show with four experts saying: this is going to be the end of all the ice in the Arctic, and hypothesizing that it was going to be the hottest summer ever. Was it hell! It was very cold and very wet and now we've seen evidence that the glaciers in Alaska have started growing rapidly — and they've not grown for a long time."

Here's another revealing quote: "The idiot fringe have accused me of being like a Holocaust denier, which is ludicrous. Climate change is all about cycles; it's a natural thing and has always happened. When the Romans lived in Britain they were growing very good red grapes and making wine on the borders of Scotland. It was evidently a lot warmer." Grapes could not now be successfully grown in northern England.

Faced with undeniable evidence that the climate is NOT warming, the global warming theory becomes unsustainable and cannot survive an outbreak of cold weather. As countries round the globe shivered in record low temperatures, many said: "Where's global warming when you need it?" Temperatures plunged round the world in 2008 and *The Daily Telegraph*, London, reported that the Alps had their best snowfalls in a generation.

In December 2008 I put this headline on our website *(www.thefreepressonline.co.uk):* "Brrr... it's global non-warming weather!" The story recounted tales of severe snowstorms in America, "the worst ice storm in a decade in Maine" and heavy snow and avalanche alerts in France.

Earlier that year I ran this headline: "Record snow, lowest temperatures in 50 years in China — must be global non-warming again!" Then in March of 2008 came this news from China: "Many trees have fallen...and the electric lines are down. It is as if we had suffered an aerial attack or lost a battle. This is a terrible disaster. We're hungry and cold." This came via the *Daily Reckoning's* Buenos Aires correspondent, Horacio Pozzo. He goes on to tell us: "China has suffered in the last few weeks a severe crisis, with temperatures at their lowest levels in 50 years and record snowfalls. Energy shut-offs, water shortages, supplies of food running out, millions of people trapped, unable to produce or buy...creating an unimaginable paralysis... exposing to the world China's extreme fragility...

"Unshakable and powerful China has succumbed not to recession, nor to economic slowdown... but to nature. Something much more powerful... and against which there is no Bernanke, no lower rates, no more liquidity, no Buffett, no credit insurance... nothing to save us."

I could fill this book with such stories. But many are archived on our website, *www.thefreepressonline.co.uk* and if you key in "global non-warming"on our search engine, you can read them yourselves as a sort of claptrap antidote, in case you've been watching too much politically correct television. What you have seen about global warming is one-sided and inaccurate, for global warming is a myth.

Just as predictions of desert-like conditions for Britain didn't survive the next summer's non-stop deluge, global-non-warming has evolved to keep the people's attention and promote massive government interference in our lives.

Here's how Britain's *The Independent* newspaper reported on the alleged Sahara-style threat to our gardens. The headline was "Now climate change is threatening the traditional cottage garden," by Terry Kirby, Chief Reporter: Wednesday, 13 September, 2006. The story read:

"The quintessential English garden is under threat from climate change and gardeners must adapt or see their plots wither and die from the effects of hotter summers and dry winters. New types of drought-resistant Mediterranean plants, restricted water use and imaginative garden design would all have to become part of the gardens of the future, Ian Pearson, the environment and climate change minister, warned yesterday.

"Speaking at the Royal Botanic Gardens at Kew in south-west London, Mr. Pearson said: 'The quintessential English garden is under threat [and] will have to adapt to our changing climate. Gardeners have a responsibility in water use, species type and garden design to adapt too.'"

Wrong, dead wrong! The BBC reported the next summer, 2007, as follows: "Summer weather wettest on record." The BBC said that in the three months to July 23 more than 15.2 inches of rain fell on England and Wales, making it the wettest period since records began 240 years earlier! All those cacti that gardening and climate "experts" were urging people to plant, to cope with the droughts to come, no doubt rotted in the ensuing deluge. It was as if God was teaching people a lesson and I laughed as I looked out at the sheets of rain pelting down daily.

Faced with all these obvious contradictions: they say it's getting hotter, but it isn't; they say it's getting dryer, but it isn't; they say sea levels are rising, but they aren't; how do you keep this lucrative "climate con" running? For the show must go on, as so many characters want their appearance fees. Easy. You change the title to "climate change". So, cold winters weren't a sign of warming, but of global climate change. The misinformation reads like this: mankind is burning too much fossil fuel, so the cold gets colder and the heat gets hotter. The wet gets wetter. The dry gets dryer. And the confusion gets what? More confusing. No matter what the evidence is, goes the argument, it's all climate change. And that, of course, means that the government must step in with spurious solutions. They say: "Trust us. We're experts from the government. We're going to help you." Hop aboard the Climate Change Railway Express, steaming ahead while burning trillions of dollars in its firebox.

As always, follow the money. The real global glitch is that scientists do not get research grants if they say there is no major man-made problem with the weather. No research grant if Prof says there is nothing much we can influence by our behaviour.

The question behind all this is — what's in it for the governments that they so desperately want to push the scare stories of climate change? What do they get out of it? The bottom line is government control. If climate change was a real threat, then we would have to accept global rules, global governance etc — or else we would all be doomed. If the population as a whole could be convinced the planet was really in danger, people would have to accept almost anything to "save the world." Unfortunately, people question very little of what they are told, and the media have failed to keep people fully informed. They have not been "fair and balanced"; they have not presented both sides; they have not asked the hard questions; they have not done the basic research.

Research literature pours out of universities, strongly in favor of "doing something" about climate change. Politicians use this to justify doing what they've always aimed at: rebuilding the world into a socialist superstate, the coming New World Order. All carbon-based energy is demonized, whether idiocies like windmill power work or not. "Green energy", in particular using corn to make gasoline, doesn't have to make practical or financial sense, because what we are seeing is a crusade, not economic reality. It is a false belief system, which is why we have included it in this book. (I am in favor of some "green" energy projects, like geothermal heat for buildings, which makes perfect sense.)

So there is the massive attack on our industries and energy supplies on the lines of: wind good, coal bad, even though for every battery of windmills there has to be a conventional power station on standby for when the wind stops blowing.

All this is because we are told we have to stop sea levels rising, lest assorted islanders get washed off their atolls. But are sea levels really rising? Like global warming, it's one of the world's greatest lies. To justify spending trillions combating (non existent) global warming, it is claimed that, around the world, whole swathes of countries like The Maldives are likely to disappear 'neath the waves. Blah blah blah. Fortunately, it's all tosh. People often question my statements on this, so please do some sceptical research of your own and find the facts — the facts big media will seldom broadcast. Some people, however, try to print the truth.

One of the great reporters of our times is Christopher Booker of *The Sunday Telegraph* and in 2009 he interviewed Dr. Nils-Axel Mörner, who demolished the idea that the Antarctic and Greenland ice caps will melt, warming oceans will expand, and the result will be catastrophe. Remember Al Gore — the well known internet inventor and all round blowhard, who talks in his film *An Inconvenient Truth*, of a sea level rise of 20 feet. In this film the ice sheets over cities have been replaced by sheets of water. Oh dear.

Wrote Christopher Booker: "If there is one scientist who knows more about sea levels than anyone else in the world, it is the Swedish geologist and physicist Nils-Axel Mörner, formerly chairman of the IN-QUA International Commission on Sea Level Change. And the uncompromising verdict of Dr. Mörner, who for 35 years has been using every known scientific method to study sea levels all over the globe, is that all this talk about the sea rising is nothing but a colossal scare story.

"Despite fluctuations down as well as up, 'the sea is not rising,' he says. 'It hasn't risen in 50 years.' If there is any rise this century, it will 'not be more than 10cm (four inches), with an uncertainty of plus or minus 10 cm.' And quite apart from examining the hard evidence, he says, the elementary laws of physics (latent heat needed to melt ice) tell us that the apocalypse conjured up by Al Gore and Co could not possibly come about."

He adds that Dr. Mörner, formerly a Stockholm professor, knows all the warmist propaganda is wrong as it is all based on computer model predictions. His own findings are based on "going into the field to observe what is actually happening in the real world."

Adds Mr. Booker: "When running the International Commission on Sea Level Change, he launched a special project on the Maldives, whose leaders have for 20 years been calling for vast sums of international aid to stave off disaster."

- Six times Dr. Morner's experts visited the islands, to confirm that the sea has not risen for half a century. He offered to show the inhabitants a film explaining why they had nothing to worry about. The government refused to let it be shown.
- In Tuvalu, whose politicians are demanding their people be evacuated, the sea has, if anything, dropped in recent decades. Meanwhile, Venice has been sinking rather than the Adriatic rising, says Dr. Mörner.

Concluded Mr. Booker: "One of his most shocking discoveries was why the IPCC has been able to show sea levels rising by 2.3mm a year. Until 2003, even its own satellite-based evidence showed no upward trend. But suddenly the graph tilted upwards because the IPCC's favoured experts had drawn on the finding of a single tide-gauge in Hong Kong harbor showing a 2.3 mm rise. The entire global sea-level projection was then adjusted upwards by a "corrective factor" of 2.3 mm, because, as the IPCC scientists admitted, they "needed to show a trend.""

For more information, see Dr Mörner on *YouTube* (Google Mörner, Maldives and YouTube); or read on the net his 2007 EIR interview "Claim that sea level is rising is a total fraud"; or email him morner@pog.nu — to buy a copy of his booklet, *'The Greatest Lie Ever Told.'* Also of interest is a book which Christopher Booker co/wrote with Richard North: *Scared to Death: From BSE to Global Warming: Why Scares are Costing Us the Earth.*

Fortunately, the earth is the Lord's and everything in it. It spins at His command and will continue to do so for as long as He wills it. And it spins at the temperature He decides! Catastrophe IS coming to the world, and to find out about that you have to study Bible prophecy or buy our books and DVDs from our website, ***thefreepressonline.co.uk.*** Fortunately, there is also a Savior of the world. He is coming back soon — and His name is not Al Gore.

Chapter 14

Table of Truth:
Bahai vs. the Bible

This is a cult which came out of Islam.

Started by: "The Bab", a Muslim merchant in Persia (Iran) in 1844, who proclaimed that a messenger of God was coming. That was Baha'u'llah.

Founded by: Persian Muslim Baha'u'llah, who claimed to be a prophet.

Numbers: Five to six million.

Headquarters: Haifa, Israel.

They deny the deity of Christ and say that the Lord Jesus was a prophet for His time, but was superseded by Baha'u'llah.

Bahai says:	The Bible says:
God	**God**
One God for all men of all religions. No trinity.	Almighty God, Three Persons in One God, approachable only through God the Son, the Lord Jesus Christ.
Goals	**Goals**
Peace on earth; end of all war; unification of all religions; unity of all people in peace under a one world government; exaltation of work as a form of worship; the establishment of a universal	The Bible teaches that there will be world peace, but not until the true Messiah, the Lord Jesus, returns, when the kingdom of God will be established. "Thy kingdom come" will be literally fulfilled.

Bahai says:	The Bible says:
language to unify the world; an international "force" to back the one world government.	In the meantime, Christians are to spread the good news of salvation for all who will trust in the Lord Jesus for forgiveness of sins.
The Lord Jesus	**The Lord Jesus**
Jesus was a prophet for His time only; His death was not significant and was not a sacrifice for sin.	Savior of the world, who died to pay the price for all our sin, for all those who will accept Him as their Lord.
Heaven and hell	**Heaven and hell**
Figments of the imagination.	Eternal life with the Lord or torment without end in hell.
Messiah	**Messiah**
The Bahai messiah is the Baha'u'llah.	Messiah of Israel, Savior of the world, the Holy One, is the Lord Jesus, our blessed Redeemer.
Capital city	**Capital city**
Haifa, Israel, the location of the Shrine of the Bab, on the slopes of Mt. Carmel.	Jerusalem, not Haifa, is the Lord's special city, from which He will reign on the earth during the 1,000 year (Millennium).
Prophet	**Prophet**
The Bahai religion was started by a Persian merchant, a Muslim who gave himself the title Bab (gate) and prophesied that a messenger of God (Baha'u'llah) was coming.	"And many false prophets shall rise; and shall deceive many." Matthew 24:11
Shrine	**Shrine**
The Bahai headquarters and Shrine of the Bab, high on Mount Carmel overlooking Haifa bay, features beautiful gardens descending in terraces down the	Christians need no shrines; we are temples of the Holy Spirit. We need no earthly HQ. We ARE the HQ.

Bahai says:	The Bible says:
mountain. Bahais from all over the world give their time and money to keep these gardens beautiful.	
Scripture	**Scripture**
The Bible is not the final authority; the writings of Baha'u'llah are new revelation from God.	"All scripture is given by inspiration of God, and is profitable for doctrine, for reproof, for correction, for instruction in righteousness." 2 Tim 3:16. The canon of scripture is closed.
Holy Book	**Holy Book**
The Baha'u'llah's teaching is in a book called the Kitab'l'Aqdas, plus many other books.	The Bible, God's Word, written over about 1,500 years by 40 men inspired by the Holy Spirit, verified by over 100 fulfilled prophecies, by mountains of archaeological evidence, and by 2,000 years of faithful witness of millions of lives transformed by the power of the gospel.

We spent five weeks in Haifa visiting family and every day we had to walk past the Shrine of the Bab. There was always activity there, with coachloads of tourists arriving to view the shrine and the famous terraced gardens. A local man told us that Bahais were expecting the Baha'u'llah to return on a ship to Haifa harbour, walk up Ben Gurion Street and then on up through the steep terraces and into the shrine.

The religion has an appeal to people concerned about world peace. In the light of Bible prophecy, it is rather chilling to find that Bahai goals are the joining of all religions and one world government. You can be of any religion and join the Bahais. Any religion, that is, except true Christianity! How sad for these people when they find that their faith has been misplaced.

Chapter 15

Warning:
False Faiths and Dangerous Practices
by Pat Franklin

Psychic circles

We fell for this in the 1970s, before we came to faith in the Lord. We knew a couple, both psychic mediums, who claimed to have a healing ministry. They invited us to develop our "psychic abilities" by joining their development circle one evening a week. This consisted of sitting in a circle in a dark room for about an hour, clearing our minds and just waiting for something to happen. Nothing much ever did happen (thank you, Lord!). One time someone claimed they saw a light. Another time someone said they saw a picture of mustard and a knife cutting it. Then one evening the leader said he had heard "the friends" moving about outside the door. By "the friends" he meant spirit beings. This was very stupid indeed, because we could all hear someone moving outside the door, and we all knew it was his teenage son, who was roller skating around the house the entire evening. The room we met in was the couple's healing room, where they prayed for the sick. On one wall was a huge picture of a full size Shroud of Turin.

One Thursday evening we turned up for the development circle and the wife met us at the door of their large, expensive home in the city of Winchester, England. As she opened the door she said: "Oh, Alan and Pat — you are going to expose us one day." Then she smiled and welcomed us in, as if she hadn't heard what she just said. We did not remark on this at all. We sat in the circle, nothing happened, we all had a cup of tea and said goodnight. As soon as we got out into our car, we looked at each other and said: "Did you hear what V___ said? She said we're going to expose them!" And we agreed that she might well be right, because we had found out that, apart from anything else, the couple were not honest with money. The couple are both dead now, and we do not name them in print for the sake of their children.

This book is it; this is the exposé! The "friends", the spirit beings which that couple could sometimes contact, were not friends at all, but demonic beings masquerading as the spirits of dead people. By their fruits you will know them, the Lord Jesus said. The fruit was not good, not good at all. There was fruit, and it was all rotten. You mess with these occult things at your peril. We just thank the Lord that He rescued us out of all this, but even then, we did not get away scot free. We paid a price for our involvement, even though it was done in ignorance, and we would urge everyone to steer well clear of any involvement in anything psychic. No good will come of it. Even if you seem to gain some advantage or some healing, it will turn very sour indeed.

Here is a list of just some of the rotten fruit we know of in the lives of real people as a result of psychic dabbling: bad health; bad decisions; immorality; unstable marriages; broken homes; birth defects; poverty; insanity. A very nasty list indeed. Someone has written that dabbling in the occult is like a baby being allowed to play in a sewer. Or it is like playing with fire. You will certainly be burnt.

Remember, psychic equals occult and the occult is the dark supernatural. It is real. It can hurt you. It can destroy you and those you love. We urge all readers to renounce any past involvement with things psychic and to go through their homes with a fine tooth comb and get rid of anything to do with the occult. We did. We burned books; we threw out anything that belonged to that dark realm. A partial list of things to weed out: books on astrology, horoscopes, witchcraft or spells; all horoscope items; religious tribal art items including dreamcatchers; statues or pictures of Buddha; statues of saints; pictures of saints; rosaries; scapulars; any object that is venerated in any way including posters of the Shroud of Turin; good luck charms; hex signs. Clear the decks!

Ask our Father in the name of the Lord Jesus Christ to forgive you for any occult involvement and to cleanse you and protect you. He will certainly answer that prayer, for that is why Jesus came:

"For this purpose was the Son of God manifested: that He might destroy the works of the devil..."   1 John 3:8

False religion is like an octopus with dozens or even hundreds of tentacles, but one head, and that head is Satan, so we finish with a dread roll call of a few other movements and false religions to watch out for. This is by no means comprehensive, and new tentacles are probably forming as this book goes to the printer.

The Emerging Church

This is the latest we know of, and is still taking shape. It seems to be drawing people from Protestant churches who want to experience something with their senses. They want altars, statues, pictures, incense, candles, vestments. In a word, back to Rome. If that is the final shape of this movement, obviously it is a betrayal of the Bible and is heading in the wrong direction.

Hinduism

Hindus have millions of idols which they think represent gods. They choose which ones they want to worship. We have been in Hindu homes where they have china cabinets containing the little statues of their favourite gods. They pray to these things, but the Bible says they are praying to devils and that idol images of so-called gods have demons attached to them.

"Wherefore, my dearly beloved, flee from idolatry."
1 Corinthians 10:14

"But I say, that the things which the gentiles sacrifice, they sacrifice to devils, and not to God: and I would not that ye should have fellowship with devils. Ye cannot drink the cup of the Lord, and the cup of devils: ye cannot be partakers of the Lord's table, and of the table of devils."
1 Corinthians 10:20, 21

We know one Hindu family, all of whom came to know the Lord Jesus as their Savior. They collected up all the family "gods", some of which were made of gold or silver, and destroyed them all. Hallelujah!

Buddhism

This was started by a Nepalese man who practised self denial. He became a travelling "holy man" and sat under a fig tree in India for days until he declared that he had achieved his goal of becoming a

Buddha, an "enlightened one". There could be up to five hundred million Buddhists in the world today. They believe in reincarnation and karma, the wheel of life whereby you pay in the next life for the bad things you did in this life. There is no salvation, no forgiveness. You can become a Buddha, and escape the terrible wheel of suffering only when you reach Nirvana, or the end of all craving. The pernicious teaching of karma has terrible effects. Anyone suffering poverty or sickness is seen as getting his just desserts for his bad deeds in a previous existence.

They also think you can get rid of some of the bad karma by chanting things over and over. As we have said already, this can open the mind to demonic influence.

Yoga

Yoga is NOT "just exercise". It is an eastern, pagan way to worship false gods through physical positions. For example the "Salute to the Sun" exercise done in many yoga classes is worshipping the actual sun. Not something a Christian wants to do! We worship God who made the sun; we worship the true Creator, not His creation.

In Britain practically every church hall has a yoga class meeting one evening a week. Ignorance of this is inexcusable. It is a terrible insult to God to have regular sessions of eastern worship going on in buildings paid for by people who are supposed to worship His beloved Son. Perhaps we could hold weekly gospel meetings in Hindu temples — that would be the mirror image of what is going on. Somehow I don't think the Hindus would allow our evangelists to rent their halls one night a week. They are more clued up and committed that we are! Time to wake up!

They will not tell you this at the yoga class (maybe they don't even know themselves), but yoga is to do with "serpent power", *kundalini*, the serpent which is supposedly coiled at the base of everyone's spine. Yoga exercises are designed to enable this horrible creature to rise up and into your life. This is out and out satanic.

What about the relaxation at the end of the class, surely that's got to be OK? No, because you clear your mind, you open yourself up mentally, you allow things to come into your mind — pictures, maybe a light, you follow the light... This is one of the classic ways of opening yourself to the influence of demons. Remember — Satan comes as an angel of light!

So — exercise your foot by kicking yoga out of your life! Join a gym or just do some floor exercises at home, but please, no yoga.

Hare Krishna

A being called Krishna is worshipped. Chanting the Krishna mantra is the way to achieve salvation. The followers do not work, for the most part. They beg. This is not spiritual; it is lazy. And their chanting is occult. It puts people into an altered state of consciousness in which they attract demonic influences. You see Hare Krishnas sometimes in prosperous towns like Cambridge, England. We don't give these able-bodied layabouts any money.

Wicca

This is a nature religion (Mother Earth) using magic. There are various gods and goddesses and it includes belief in reincarnation and karma. It is witchcraft in the raw, and although some would say "white" witchcraft, because one of its tenets is to do no harm, it is satanic through and through. It is accepted as a religion in U.S. courts and there are even Wiccan chaplains in some prisons. That is how far our civilization has descended.

Transcendental meditation

Blanking out the mind, trying to get into an altered state of consciousness, opening up yourself to dark spiritual forces which will masquerade as something good. The Bible kind of meditating, on the other hand, is thinking about scriptures. For example, thinking about a verse from the gospels or the psalms, turning it over in your mind. Biblical meditation is active, not passive. You do not turn your brain off; you keep it fully on, thinking about the scripture, thinking about how it relates to other scriptures, maybe thanking the Lord for it or asking Him to help you understand it more fully — things like that.

Ouija board

This is NOT a game. It is NOT harmless fun. Playing with a ouija board is an attempt to find out information, get answers, in a supernatural way. The Bible calls this *divination.* God totally forbids this, and for a very good reason — it opens the door to demonic influence. Remember, Satan will use *anything* to get a foot in the door of your life — even something that seems like a game. He can use this "game" to destroy you.

One example from real life: an American woman (no one related to us, thank the Lord!) started using the ouija board regularly, but then got scared and packed it away. It started calling her to get it out. She lost her mind. Her son became a homosexual.

An example from our own life: we've mentioned this elsewhere in the book, but before we became Christians, we played with the "game" with some other people and asked for advice on whether to invest in a certain company. We ensured that none of us could cheat and push the glass by all closing our eyes, except for the person watching the glass, and then taking turns being the one to watch the glass. It whizzed round, always spelling: "Invest more". We did, just in time for the company to run out of money (our money). We learned our lesson. God protected us and even showed us the most incredible mercy, because after a long time and much misery, we actually got our money back.

Pendulum swinging

This is one of those psychic rituals used for divination, acquiring information supernaturally. Before ultrasound, some people used to use this to try to determine the sex of unborn babies, by swinging a pendulum over the mother's abdomen. We know people who deeply regret doing this and blame it for birth defects.

Spiritual mapping in the business world

This was something we heard of at a business conference. The occult can rear its ugly head anywhere these days. A speaker claimed special power to know how to help companies map their business strategies for success. She claimed others could learn the same techniques. We wrote to the organisers of the conference warning that this was occult and totally forbidden by God. We never heard back from them.

Crystal ball gazing

This is old style witchcraft — divination, trying to get knowledge by staring at something — a crystal, or it could be tea leaves, embers of a fire etc. If you have such an object as a crystal ball, we recommend a sledgehammer…

Tarot cards

Another occult means of trying to tell the future. A sledgehammer won't work with Tarot cards, but you probably have a match…

Christian Science (Church of Christ, Scientist)

They have "reading rooms" in many towns in England. But it is NOT Christian and it is NOT scientific.

As with so many cults, it was started by a deluded woman, Mary Baker Eddy. The year was 1879. She taught that illness was just an illusion, so you did not need doctors. But she was a hypocrite, and sought medical treatment when she needed it. Her final illness was not an illusion, and she died, and you can see the rather nice houses where she lived in New Hampshire and Massachusetts. She believed she was the woman of Revelation 12 and that she alone had the key to interpreting the Bible. Wrong again! Mary died of her illusory illness in 1910. She had the gall to charge people $300.00 for a few healing lessons, and died a millionaire.

Scientology

L. Ron Hubbard, a science fiction writer, started this to make money, and it worked. The goal is to become a "Clear" and to become clear, you have to go through several stages, and guess what, each stage is going to cost you. It will clear out your bank account all right!

Quakers

We attended one of their meetings years ago. About 10 people, mostly elderly, sat in a circle for about 30 minutes and no one said a word. Then we all went home. Very peaceful, to the point of being boring, and not at all Christian. Not one word about the Lord Jesus, His atoning sacrifice, the need to be born again etc.

Unitarian

They believe in morality, but do not accept the deity of the Lord Jesus, so hell opens its mouth.

Rosicrucianism

Mystical esoteric society in the Middle Ages supposedly for the enlightenment of mankind (it provided no enlightenment whatsoever). The name means "rosy cross" and it inspired an order in Freemasonry. Newspapers today carry adverts inviting people to get involved in this. We invite people to renounce it and ask the Lord Jesus to forgive them and cleanse them of all involvement.

Christadelphianism

They claim to be Christian, and they study the Bible, but deny the deity of Christ.

Kabbalah

A mystical system of interpreting everything. Among other things, it teaches that there are secrets in the shape of the Hebrew letters of the Old Testament. If only they would read and accept the plain teaching of the Bible, they would forget this nonsense. And oh yes, a little red cord tied round the wrist is just so spiritual...

Chapter 16

Are You Ready for the Rapture?
by Alan Franklin

When I first visited America, I was intrigued to see car fender stickers reading: "Are you ready for the rapture?" What was this rapture? When would it take place? Who would be involved? Today I am often asked about the rapture and challenged over its timing. Will Christians be caught away from the earth, to meet the Lord Jesus in the air? What matters is not my opinion, but what the Bible says.

I believe the rapture, the removal of the true church prior to the pending disaster, will take place before the coming seven years of tribulation — The Great Tribulation, the worst time in the world's history. It will be a real event likely to cause astonishment and consternation among those who remain. The liberal media and nominal Christians will be hard pressed to explain the disappearance of hundreds of millions of people, some from every nation on earth. One reason for UFO stories could be that Satan is getting his excuse ready: "The Christians were removed by higher beings in order to be re-educated and fitted into the coming New World Order."

So where is the rapture in scripture? First Thessalonians 4, verse 14, is clear: "...even so them also which sleep in Jesus will God bring with Him..." He cannot bring them with Him if they have not already joined Him at a previous time. Verses 16 to 18 state that we who are alive at that time shall be caught up to meet the Lord in the air. This is the coming of the Lord Jesus for His saints. The verses reveal that He is going to gather us to Himself so that subsequently He may return to earth with all of us, as the last verse of chapter 3 states.

Readers should note the distinction between the Lord coming *for* us and His coming *with* us to get a clear concept of the Lord's return. The two events are separated by more than seven years, as the church will not be on earth during the tribulation period. We will have been taken out from "the wrath to come." Never in the Bible does the church face God's wrath. The church is not mentioned after chapter three of Revelation — we are not here, although many will come to faith at this time — the tribulation saints.

Nobody knows when the rapture will happen, as God has not revealed it, although we are told what the signs of the times will be when it happens. However, no scripture needs to be fulfilled before the rapture can occur — it could be today!

So the first thing Jesus will do will be to join with His body — that is us! He is not to be Head without the body, but will catch us up to meet Him in the air. If we are dead, He will raise us; if alive, He will change us, and take us to His Father's house for the marriage of the Lamb; for this is our home; and He must have His heirs with Him.

In the Book of Revelation you first have the marriage of the Lamb, and then you see the Lamb coming out of Heaven with His armies following Him. This is when Jesus brings judgement and destruction to His enemies, the armies of Antichrist gathered round Jerusalem.

When the Lord Jesus does appear, girded for war in His role as the Lion of the Tribe of Judah, the world will see us with Him. When He meets us in the air, coming like a thief in the night, nobody but us will see Him! He will hardly come like a thief in the night at the end, when the whole world will watch in terror! These are two separate, quite distinct occasions. Otherwise the descriptions of the occasion are so contradictory it would make no sense. And the Bible makes perfect sense. The imminence of His arrival is what should keep Christians on their toes. The pre-trib rapture position Pat and I hold should encourage a strong sense of urgency and immanency. Our time is short and there is work to be done!

Many Christians will be familiar with the book and film series called "Left Behind" which topped best-seller lists. This is a fictionalised account of what happens to those who come to belief after the rapture and served to wake many people up. As the books pointed out, a lot of people who think they are Christians will be left on earth. Some will subsequently be saved, while others will undoubtedly be bitter when they realise what has happened.

The word "rapture" is not in the Bible, but is derived from the Latin word "rapio" or "raptura," which means to be "caught up, to be snatched away." This is a translation of the Greek expression used by the Apostle Paul when he spoke of the rapture: "For the Lord himself shall descend from heaven with a shout, with the voice of the archangel, and with the trump of God: and the dead in Christ shall rise first: then we which are alive and remain shall be caught up together with them in the clouds, to meet the Lord in the air: and so shall we ever be with the Lord." *(1 Thesslalonians 4:16–18.)* No judgement of the earth is mentioned in this passage, which is significant. The event happens in the clouds, not on the earth — in contrast to the end of the Tribulation period, a drama played out on earth.

In John 14:1–3 Jesus promises that He will come back from heaven for his followers, who will then be with him for ever. No prophecy remains to be fulfilled before this astonishing event takes place. It could be tomorrow — or in 20 years' time. When the Lord Jesus comes into the atmosphere, although not to the earth itself, there will be a mighty shout to which the born again Christians will respond. The dead believers from the church age will first rise from their graves, all round the world, to go up to meet their Lord (saints from the Old Testament era will be raised at a later time). Moments later living Christians from all over the world will be hurtling upwards, exchanging their earthly bodies for perfect heavenly bodies as they go. No more wrinkles, aches and pains for them!

They will be taken out from aeroplanes, cars, buildings — from sleep and from work. Cars and buses they were driving will probably just crash and the resulting panic and carnage will shake the world. The fear and chaos could be the trigger for ushering in the one-world government. Hundreds of millions of nominal Christians who have never been born again — the vast majority of people taking the title Christian — will remain. These will include most of the bishops and leaders of all established denominations, many of whom long since ceased to believe the words of Jesus. They will be baffled and angry at a seemingly supernatural event they cannot at first explain. Even after the rapture, these people will probably never admit that this event was clearly predicted in the Bible — because that would mean that their "Christian" titles were mere shams and that they were hypocrites. Many well known leaders will be left behind and the Lord Jesus will later tell them: "I never knew you."

Is the rapture really close? I think so. Christian date-setters have come a series of embarrassing croppers, writing books with titles like:

"88 reasons the Lord will return in 1988," Colin Deal's best seller of the early 1980s. Not a lot of sales for that title now.... The date was set, I suspect, because Israel was born in 1948. Many people thought a generation was 40 years and Christ would then return, Matthew having written that this generation — the generation that saw this national rebirth — would not pass till all these things be fulfilled *(Matt 24:34)*. When date-setters constantly get things wrong, people lose all interest in the whole idea of the rapture and the Second Coming, or even deny the prophecies.

The rapture must come before the time of Jacob's troubles. Here are some verses which make that clear:

"Because thou hast kept the word of my patience, I also will keep thee from the hour of temptation, which shall come upon all the world, to try them that dwell upon the earth."

Revelation 3:10

"For God hath not appointed us to wrath, but to obtain salvation by our Lord Jesus Christ."

1 Thessalonians 5:9

In Titus 2:13 we are told to look for the blessed hope "and the glorious appearing of the great God and our Saviour Jesus Christ."

Both 1 Thessalonians and 1 Corinthians talk of a "trump" or trumpet sound. This does not refer to the seventh trumpet of Revelation, for Revelation had not been written then. Paul was talking about the blowing of trumpets at the Jewish Feast of Trumpets, taking place every year in the synagogues. The trumpets gave a short blast, the "last trump" Paul refers to. Writing in *The Chosen People Question Box 11*, Dr. Henry J. Heydt explains: "The Feast of Trumpets preceded the time of affliction portrayed by Yom Kippur *(Lev 23:24, 27)* and proves, by the application Paul gave to it, that the resurrection, change and catching away of believers (1 Thess 4:15–17) takes place before the time of Jacob's trouble."

If we are to be looking continuously for the rapture, as the Greek word *harpazo* indicates, it could happen anywhen. If the rapture is placed during or after the tribulation, these are events which would have to come first, destroying the idea of immanency. In 2 Thessalonians 2:6–8 we are told that there is a restrainer, holding back the spirit of iniquity. Antichrist cannot swagger on to the scene until God's time, when this restrainer is removed. The wicked one cannot be revealed until the Holy Spirit is removed. This could explain why all the past advertised appearances of antichrist types, like "Maitreya the Christ," widely promoted in the 1980s, failed to occur. This restrainer is the Holy Spirit, acting through His true church. When the church is removed at the rapture, it will be unseen by the world, as it happens in a fraction of a second, "the twinkling of an eye." Only then will "all hell" be permitted to be let loose on the earth. In 1 Thessalonians 1:10 Paul states that Jesus will deliver believers from the wrath to come. This wrath is in the future and cannot refer to hell, as true believers will not go to hell, Jesus having saved them by His sacrifice on the cross. The wrath refers to the Great Tribulation.

In Luke (21:36) Jesus told his disciples to pray so that if possible they might escape the horrors to come, and in Revelation, with its blow by blow account of the end times, only in chapters one to three is the church mentioned. The church is in heaven in chapter four — so cannot be on the earth on which God is pouring out judgement. God's true saints never suffer His wrath. The "tribulation saints" are those believers killed during the tribulation — the people saved during this time, in a variety of ways including listening to the preaching of 144,000 Messianic Jewish preachers. There will be a great multitude of new believers, from all nations, tribes and peoples of the earth, according to Revelation 7:9–10.

Once the Antichrist has full dominion over the earth, halfway through the seven year tribulation, he will bring in the "mark of the beast" system under which nobody can buy or sell without his mark on their right hands or foreheads. *(Revelation 13:5–7, 16–17)*. So any people coming to belief in this time will face martyrdom, by being beheaded. They will be resurrected after Christ returns with His saints and will rule with him on earth for a thousand years, the true millennium.

So there are two distinct groups of Christians; those comprising the church before the tribulation and those saved during it. The church, the bride of Christ arrayed in fine linen representing the righteousness of the saints *(Revelation 19:7–8)* returns with our Lord after seven years of tribulation on the earth, so is not there during this time. This will be at a time when the world is virtually destroyed, when all life would cease if the tumult went on any longer. Matthew wrote *(Matthew 24:21)* that unless those days be shortened no flesh should be saved... No one will be crying "peace and safety" at this point, the campaign of Armageddon.

Suppose that the rapture came at the end of the tribulation. Imagine the scene. Terrified groups of believers, hiding out in caves and woods. They were the few who had not taken the mark and had survived, living wild in remote wildernesses. Some may have heard of the two witnesses, testifying in Jerusalem. The two were then killed, the world rejoiced — and the "church" remnant knew they had another three and a half years to suffer. Armies were surrounding Jerusalem, a nuclear war was taking place — so could they possibly be slumbering and sleeping? Is this such a time "as you think not"? No, we are told that when the Lord Jesus returns, to defeat His enemies and walk again on the Mount of Olives, ALL His saints come with him, so they (we) must have been in Heaven with Him beforehand.

There are those in the west today who think they will conquer the world for Christ, then hand it, gift-wrapped, to Him on His return. They go on "Marches for Jesus," shouting out about claiming the land and singing songs of triumph and victory. Since they have been doing it, the world has been steadily getting worse. These "kingdom now," "manifest sons of God" and "name it and claim it" enthusiasts do a lot of shouting with little result. The places they claim remain unchanged and unregenerated. Sin increases, wickedness proliferates, as it will continue to do until Christ's return. There will be no great end-times revival, as many claim. The Bible instead tells of a great falling away and terrible apostasy. If you meet Christ with your feet firmly on terra firma, you are working for the Antichrist or hiding from his forces. Real Christians will leave this sin-sick world when Jesus comes calling for His bride, the church. Remember, He is Jewish. Jewish bridegrooms in the Lord's era liked to surprise their bride, by coming unexpectedly, in the middle of the night.

A study of Revelation confirms the pre-wrath rapture of the church. Revelation 3:10 states: "Because thou hast kept the word of My patience, I also will keep thee from the hour of temptation, which shall come upon all the world, to try them that dwell upon the earth." So the church has a promise — it will be kept from the trials that are about to occur on the earth, which means it must be removed first. The saints killed during the Tribulation are new believers, so the promise of safety is not theirs.

The rapture will be a devastating surprise to the world — and a marvellous one to Christians — which rules out it happening any time during the tribulation. We know when that will start — when Antichrist signs a seven year peace deal with Israel. We would then be able to work out the likely time of the rapture if it were to come in the middle or at the end of the seven years, so these theories do not stack up. Jesus would not then be coming back unexpectedly, "as a thief in the night" *(1 Thessalonians 5:1–2)*. So we can rest assured that whatever hard times we may have to face now, the Lord will take us home before that terrible seven-year period.

Israel in particular will be living a delusion, having been deceived by Antichrist and foolishly believing his promises of peace. There will be no peace until the Prince of Peace returns to Jerusalem:

> **"For when they shall say, peace and safety; then sudden destruction cometh upon them, as travail upon a woman with child; and they shall not escape. But ye, brethren, are not in darkness, that that day should overtake you as a thief."**
>
> 1 Thessalonians 5:3, 4

The people saying peace and safety will be Israelis, under the false protection of Antichrist, the leader of the Revived Roman Empire, who will have deceitfully signed a peace treaty with them. That's when sudden destruction will come upon them. The Christians, however, are not in darkness — the darkness of tribulation. The judgement is reserved for the world, not God's people. It starts when we go. God has NOT appointed us to wrath! Christians never have to face the wrath of God: salvation is a free gift and we are not put through trials to get it, although Christians do indeed face trials!

Those who claim there is no rapture, or say the idea of a rapture prior to the tribulation is a new concept, dating from the Plymouth Brethren, are wrong. Long before John Darby and the Plymouth Brethren there is strong evidence of the understanding of the coming of the Lord in two stages in the early church. The writer Ephraem the Syrian was a major theologian of the early Byzantine church who lived from 306 to 373 A.D. He or one of his disciples authored *"On the Last Times, the Antichrist and the End of the World."* This was considered important enough to be translated into several languages. Ephraem's text teaches the premillenial return of Christ and has a clear statement about the Lord returning before the tribulation to take the elect home to be with Him before the coming tribulation.

Here is what he wrote: "For all the saints and elect of God are gathered prior to the tribulation that is to come, and are taken away to the Lord lest they see the confusion that is to overwhelm the world because of our sins." Many scholars through the ages also concluded that there will be: a personal Antichrist who will rule the revived Roman Empire during the last days; a rebuilt temple; the two witnesses; and a literal Great Tribulation.

Now, turning to the New Testament, here are a few passages to lift your hearts:

"...the coming of the Lord draweth nigh."   James 5:8

"...waiting for the coming of our Lord Jesus Christ..."
                                              1 Corinthians 1:7

"When He shall come to be glorified in His saints, and to be admired..."   1 Thessalonians 1:10

"Looking for that blessed hope, and the glorious appearing of the great God and our Savior Jesus Christ..."   Titus 2:13

"...unto them that look for Him shall He appear the second time ..."   Hebrews 9:28

These scriptures indicate that the coming of the Lord could happen at any time. If the rule of Antichrist, the Great Tribulation and the beast system — 666 and the mark — had to come first, it would be impossible for Christ to come at an unexpected time.

What we must remember is to be ready, so as not to be ashamed when the Lord comes. It should not make us complacent, for it is a purifying, motivating thought that it could be very soon. This could be the last generation to live in a sin-filled world, so the time to act is now. Make sure your own heart is pure — and witness to your unsaved loved ones. You could buy them a copy of this book!

Chapter 17

What Should You Tell Your Kids About "Santa"?
Pat Franklin gives a mother's view[1]

What do you tell your children about Christmas? Here is a picture of our daughter Annie when she was about four or five. At about this age she came home from school one day, stood in the kitchen and said: 'Someone at school said there is no Santa Claus. Is that true?'

I took a deep breath. Was I going to tell my beloved little girl a big fat lie? She would believe whatever I told her. Would she collapse in tears if I told her the truth? Would she miss out on the fun of childhood and be scarred for life and resent me for spoiling her fun? She looked up at me expectantly. She was interested. She wanted to know.

Annie, now 26, was about four years old when this picture was taken and she wanted to know the truth about 'Santa'.

I told her: "Annie, Santa Claus is like a fairy tale. There is no real Santa Claus; it's just pretend, just a story. Mom and Dad give you your presents on Christmas. But Jesus is real. Everything you learned about Jesus is true and really happened."

Her reaction? "Oh, OK." And she skipped off happily to play with her toys. Sigh of relief on my part. It did not phase her one bit. I thank

[1] This is an article which first appeared in our Free Press Online web newspaper, *www.thefree-pressionline.co.uk.*

God today that she heard the truth as soon as she tried to find it.

Several years later, she came home one day and told me: "We were talking about Christmas today and someone said there was no Santa Claus, and X (a girl her age) was shocked and said she still believed in Santa. Everybody told her that was silly and she was really upset. The girl said her mother had lied to her about it and she would never believe anything she said again."

Dear readers, it will not harm your children to know the truth. Why not tell them the whole truth this year by reading the story of Jesus' birth in the gospels of Matthew and Luke. You could spread this out over several evenings. Let the family all sit quietly together while the truth is read out. It will do your children more good than a thousand presents.

And let there be debate about it. Allow them to question it; allow them their doubts, but try to settle the doubts; try to get to the bottom of it and settle in your own mind what the truth is. The Christian faith is sound and provable — it is not a leap in the dark. 'Let us reason together,' says God in the Bible. He has given you a marvelous brain so that you can actually come to know Him, and be intellectually convinced — because there is actual, factual proof. Christianity is not like the other religions which make claims but have no proof.

God is not a mythical figure like "Santa". God has given us ample proof by the many fulfilled prophecies written down hundreds of years before the events they predict; and more proof in the miracles of the Lord Jesus — particularly His resurrection, documented and attested to by the apostles, who died martyrs' deaths rather than recant their testimonies.

I am assuming you have a Bible to read from. If not, there are often low priced Bibles at charity shops. Why not also get a good commentary that you can consult to help answer hard questions? My favorite commentary is William Macdonald's *Believer's Bible Commentary*. It could not be more clear, simple and yet deep. You can order one from a bookshop or on Amazon and it will be the best present you have ever given yourself! It is also a *great* present to give someone else for a birthday, graduation etc.

While Santa is a lie, the word is an anagram of Satan, the Father of Lies. Funny how we give so much prominence to Santa every year, but liberals deny the existence of Satan. Unfortunately, Satan, unlike Santa, is real. And as for the *Claus*, well Satan would just love to get his claws into any of us...

Jesus is true. In fact He is The Truth. He said: 'I am the way (to Heaven), the truth and the life.' When you believe the truth (by believing in Him), you will be amazed to find that you get eternal life (His guarantee of Heaven). He gives it as a free gift to all who put their trust in Him. Now that is a gift indeed. Make sure you and your children get that gift this year.

Postscript:

Annie is now married, with a little girl of her own, called Rachel. Rachel will not be told silly stories about "Santa".

Chapter 18

Some Things Every Christian
Should Know

The Bible

The religions examined in this book all have foundational books of their own. We believe the Bible is special, and we will attempt to tell you why this is.

The Holy Bible is a library of 66 books written by 40 authors over about 1,500 years. It is true history. It tells us both the past and the future. It begins with the creation of the universe and tells us what lies ahead. It is a true account of God's dealings with man from the creation of the world.

It tells the story of how God selected one man, Abraham, to be the father of a chosen people, a unique nation of people we now call the Jews. It reveals that from that nation came the Messiah, the Holy One of Israel, the Savior, the Redeemer of mankind — the God-man Jesus Christ, who died as the one and only sacrifice for the sins of all who put their faith in Him. It clearly teaches that He is to return at a certain time in history and it distinctly tells us to be ready when He comes again and gives us many signs of when that will occur. Those signs are all around us now.

The Bible is full of true accounts of kings, priests, prophets, military men, and hundreds of ordinary people. It gives great detail about the fate of specific cities, kingdoms, armies, and the rise and fall of nations. It is factually accurate and has been verified in many ways, including by archaeology. The Bible tells us that the men who wrote the scriptures were inspired by the Holy Spirit, and that even if the heavens and the earth pass away, not one word will be lost. The Bible is the most important thing in this world. It not only tells us the past and the future, but it clearly tells us how we can attain eternal life — through faith in Jesus Christ. In addition to all this, it is the greatest masterpiece of literature in all of history. It truly is "the most valuable thing this world affords."*

If you will read the Bible regularly, although each of the writers has a different style, you should actually come to know how God thinks and feels. Just read it for yourself — without any of the "study aids" supplied by different cults. The Bible is the real thing, and once you get to know the real thing better, you will be able to recognize counterfeits a mile off.

We know a mail carrier (a postman in Britain) who has read through the Bible 72 times. He is more knowledgeable in the Scriptures than most priests, bishops, archbishops — certainly more knowledgeable than the Pope! He is the fruit of what John Wycliffe began when he first translated the Scriptures into English in the 1380s. Wycliffe's famous quote to an angry cleric was: "I will make the boy that drives the plough to know more of Scripture than thou." Now anyone can read the scriptures in English, a freedom that was purchased by the blood of many martyrs.

*… "the most valuable thing this world affords." This is the phrase used by Surrey County Council's Education Committee on the flyleaf of a Bible given out to teenagers in state schools in England in 1960.

Jesus is God

When you encounter someone who denies the deity of Christ, possibly on your own doorstep, be ready to contend for the faith. Write some scripture references down at the front of your Bible so you can quickly turn to them. Here are a few scriptures:

"In the beginning was the Word, and the Word was with God, and *the Word was God*. The same was in the beginning with God."   John 1:1, 2

"All things were made by Him (the Lord Jesus); and without Him was not any thing made that was made."   John 1:3

"In Him was life…"   John 1:4

"My Lord and my God." Thomas worships the risen Lord
Jesus and Jesus accepts his worship."   1 John 20:28

The First Commandment

"I am the Lord thy God...thou shalt have *no other gods*
before Me."   Exodus 20:2, 3; Deuteronomy 5:6, 7

Since the Lord Jesus was and is and will be worshipped on earth and in
heaven, He is God. There are to be **no other gods**, none.

In the Old Testament:

"...a virgin shall conceive and bear a son, and shall call his
name Immanuel (God with us)."   Isaiah 7:14

"For unto us a child is born, unto us a son is given: and the
government shall be upon his shoulder: and his name shall be
called Wonderful, Counsellor, *The mighty God,* The everlasting Father, The Prince of Peace."   Isaiah 9:6

In the epistles:

"Looking for that blessed hope, and the glorious appearing of
the great God and our Saviour Jesus Christ..."

Titus 2:13

"That at the name of Jesus every knee should bow, of things
in heaven, and things in earth, and things under the earth:
and that every tongue should confess that Jesus Christ is
Lord, to the glory of God the Father."

Philippians 2:9–11

It gives the Father *glory* when we worship His Son!

"...he saith, And let all the angels of God *worship* him."

Hebrews 1:6

"For we shall all stand before the judgment seat of Christ.
For it is written (in Isaiah 45:23), as I live saith the LORD,
every knee shall bow to me, and every tongue shall confess to
God. So then every one of us shall give account of himself to
God."   Romans 14:10–12

"....that in all things He might have the pre-eminence. For it
pleased the Father that in Him should all fullness dwell."

Colossians 1:18, 19

In the Book of Revelation:

> **"And every creature which is in heaven, and on the earth, and under the earth, and such as are in the sea, and all that are in them, heard I saying, Blessing, and honor, and glory, and power, be unto Him that sitteth upon the throne, and unto the Lamb forever and ever."**

Revelation 5:13

The Father and the Son are worshipped together in heaven.

The Pharisees of Jesus' day knew that He was claiming to be God, and they totally rejected Him. People today in the cults are doing the same thing.

Time to be baptized!

The last words of the Lord Jesus recorded in Matthew's gospel are these: "Go ye therefore and teach all nations, baptizing them in the name of the Father and of the Son, and of the Holy Ghost: teaching them to observe all things whatsoever I have commanded you: and lo, I am with you always, even unto the end of the world."

If you have come to faith in the Lord Jesus, you need to be baptized, immersed in water, in the name of the Father and of the Son, and of the Holy Ghost. It is an act of obedience to the Lord and by it you identify yourself with the Lord Jesus in His death. As He died for you and was buried, you are briefly buried in the waters of baptism.

We marvel that a believer would hesitate to obey the Lord in this, yet we have met people who have been going to good churches for years and still are not baptized. As the years go by, they become embarrassed to admit that in fact they have never gone through the waters of baptism. This is just foolish pride. People in your church will rejoice with you when you are publicly baptized, and what a witness it will be to others who may also be hanging back. This will take guts, but if you are a believer, you can do it!

Then there are the women who do not want to have their hair-do wrecked by going underwater; they are afraid to be seen not looking their best. This is just one of the wiles of Satan, one way he keeps women from obeying the Lord's clear will — for all believers to be baptized in water. Ladies — no one minds about your hair! It is only your pride that stands in the way. The other ladies of the church will have a hair dryer handy in a back room and they will get such joy from helping you to look your best in moments. Will you not put the Lord's will first in your life?

And then there are the people who can't swim, and are afraid that they will drown. We guarantee — you will not drown! No one has ever drowned while being baptized and you will not be the first. And even if you did drown, wow, what a way to go — while submitting to a command of the Lord Jesus! But, you won't drown.

And then there are the elderly people who think they are too old — or their churches think they are too old. Praise the Lord for Rose Machin, a lady at our church. She was saved at the age of 85 and wanted to be baptized at a church in Australia. She made the arduous trip, a 23 hour flight, only to find that the large charismatic church in Sydney thought she was too old to be baptized! Back she came to England. We knew the Lord wanted this indomitable lady to go through those waters and publicly identify with the Lord Jesus in His death, so at the age of 87, Rose was baptized at Tongham Christian Fellowship. No, she did not drown or have a heart attack. Yes, her hair-do was utterly wrecked, but we had a hair dryer handy — no problem! And there was a lot of rejoicing. Rose was so glad to follow the Lord's will in this that she arranged a buffet lunch to be served to the whole church following the baptism. One of the ladies filmed the baptism, and emailed it to Australia, so the rejoicing went round the world!

God is not finished with Israel

There is a pervasive and pernicious teaching in many, even most, churches today — it is called Replacement Theology, the idea that God is finished with Israel and that the church has replaced Israel. It is just plain wrong, and it opens the door to anti-semitism.

A Jewish friend in Israel said wryly: "They take the 'good' scriptures, the promises to bless Israel, and substitute the church for Israel, but as for the 'bad' scriptures that call down judgement on Israel, those they leave for us, the Jews; they don't apply those to the church."

In Romans 11 Paul says: "Hath God cast away His people (Israel)? God forbid. For I also am an Israelite, of the seed of Abraham, of the tribe of Benjamin. God hath **not** cast away His people..." He tells us that there is a remnant of Jews saved and that the separation between us and the Jews has a purpose — to make them jealous! And Paul reveals that "blindness in part" has happened to Israel "until the fullness of the gentiles be come in." When the last gentile to be saved has been converted, wow, hang on to your hats, because: "And so all Israel shall be saved." Romans 11:26. Israel is only in the background for awhile, although of course many individual Jews are being saved.

But the day is coming when the entire nation of Israel will turn to Christ, and that is when He will return, fulfilling His prophecy:

"Ye shall not see Me henceforth, till ye shall say, Blessed is He that cometh in the name of the Lord."   Matthew 23:39

That is the time of Zechariah 12:10 when: "…they shall look upon Me whom they have pierced and they shall mourn for Him, as one mourneth for his only son…"

The world will be a very different place once the Jews have accepted their Messiah, for, as Paul says:

"If the fall of them (Israel) be the riches of the world, and the diminishing of them the riches of the gentiles, how much more their fullness?"`   Romans 11:12

"If the casting away of them be the reconciling of the world, what shall the receiving of them be, but life from the dead?"   Romans 11:15

There are surprising numbers of Jews coming to faith in Christ in our generation. Friends reckon there are about 8–10,000 Christian Jews in Israel now. There are also many Arabs coming to faith, including many in Israel. This is a wonderful thing to behold, as Arab Christians do not hate Jews, but want to bless them and bless Israel.

So, far from God being finished with Israel, He is just about to concentrate on them! They are the focus of the final seven years of this present set-up. After the church is taken up, Daniel's seventieth week, the last seven years, begins (Daniel 9:24–27). This is that awful period, known in the Bible sometimes as "the time of Jacob's trouble", sometimes as "the Day of the Lord", sometimes as the Great Tribulation. Antichrist will attempt to wipe out the Jewish people once again, as Satan has tried to do throughout history. But at the end of those terrible seven years, worse even than the Holocaust, the entire nation of Israel, every Jewish person left alive, will turn in faith to the Messiah they rejected, and that is all He is waiting for! The Lord Jesus, Lion of the tribe of Judah, will return in power and glory and majesty to rescue His beloved people Israel.

So please, never say "God is finished with the Jews." The best is yet to come — they will be helping the Lord Jesus to run the world in the 1,000 year Millennium! All the promises God made to the Jews from the time of Abraham will be fulfilled. God is not a liar! He keeps His promises. He does not promise someone something and then give it away to somebody else. We, the gentiles, are grafted in to the olive tree (a metaphor for Israel), but Paul says not to be proud about this, but fear, and

"God is able to graft them (the Jews) in again."

Romans 11:23

The Jewish people, the descendents of Abraham, will have their land, undisputed, and it will be a lot bigger territory than at present. Their numbers will be as the sand of the sea and the stars of the sky. Israel will be the head, not the tail; their light will come; the glory of the Lord will rise upon them; "gentiles shall come to thy light, and kings to the brightness of thy rising." Everlasting joy will be upon their heads and everyone on earth will acknowledge that "they are the seed which the Lord has blessed." And for Jerusalem's sake, the Lord will not rest and Israel will be a crown of glory in the hand of the Lord and the holy people there shall be called the redeemed of the Lord. (See these promises in Genesis chapters 17 and 22 and Isaiah chapters 61 and 62.)

God finished with the Jews? He's just about to start the final act. The curtain is going up. If you have never blessed the Jews, consider carefully now, for that is one way you can get in on all this glory to come. One promise to Abraham lets us get in on the act: "I will bless them that bless thee…" There may not be much time left in which to benefit from this investment opportunity…

Real estate — the land of Israel

Here is what God has to say about the land.

"…unto thy seed will I give this land."

Genesis 12:7 to Abraham

"For all the land which thou seesst, to thee will I give it, and to thy seed forever."   Genesis 13:15

"Arise, walk through the land in the length of it and in the breadth of it; for I will give it unto thee."   Genesis 13:17

"And he said unto him, I am the Lord that brought thee out of Ur of the Chaldees, to give thee this land to inherit it."

Genesis 15:7

"In the same day the Lord made a covenant with Abraham, saying: Unto they seed have I given this land, from the river

of Egypt unto the great river, the river Euphrates."

Genesis 15:18

"Sarah thy wife shall bear thee a son indeed, and thou shalt call his name Isaac: and I will establish My covenant with him for an everlasting covenant, and with his seed after him."

Genesis 17:19

"...for in Isaac shall thy seed be called."   Genesis 21:12

"...for unto thee, and unto thy seed, I will give all these countries..."   Genesis 26:3, 4 to Isaac

"...the land whereon thou liest, to thee will I give it, and to thy seed..."   Genesis 28:13 to Jacob

"And the land which I gave Abraham and Isaac, to thee I will give it, and to thy seed after thee will I give the land."

Genesis 35:12

Those who part the land (divide it, give bits of it away)

"The land shall not be sold... for the land is mine..."

Leviticus 25:23

"I will also gather all nations (*for judgement, for they have*)... parted my land."   Joel 3:2

"He (Antichrist) ...shall divide the land for gain."

Daniel 11:39

Mary

We love Mary. We expect to see her one day in heaven. But she is NOT co-redemptrix! There is ONE redeemer and it is not Mary!

When Mary was trying to get through the crowd to see the Lord Jesus, his disciples told Him His mother was outside with His half-brothers. Here is what the Lord Jesus said: "Who is my mother? And who are my brethren? And He stretched forth His hand toward His disciples, and said, Behold my mother and my brethren! For whosoever shall do the will of my Father which is in heaven, the same is my brother, and sister, and mother." Matthew 12:48–50

If you are doing the Father's will, you are as close to the Lord Jesus as if you were His mother, His brother or His sister. He said so Himself. We are not to put *anyone* on a pedestal, not Mary, not Peter, not anyone.

Judging[1]

"Don't judge, or you'll be judged!" This is often used to gag Christians, and it is taken out of context. Never let anyone stop you using your brain — your God given critical abilities to judge the truth of a matter. The New Testament was written in Greek and there are five Greek words for *judging*. Three types of judging we are *commanded* to do. *Krino* (pronounced cree-no) is the root word in most cases for judging. *Krites* (pronounced cry-teez) is Greek for a judge or magistrate.

Three kinds of judging we are commanded to do. These are:

Ana-krino — to discern

Dia-krino —— to decide on a matter

Kritikos — to critically examine and analyse

Two types of judging we are forbidden to do. These are:

Hypo-crites — judging hypocritically

Krisis — deciding who goes to heaven and who goes to hell

We would urge readers to jot these five words down at the front of their Bibles, so that the next time someone tries to gag you and stop you questioning a wrong teaching or practice, you can show them that we are *supposed* to be judging things.

Ana-krino — to discern.

"But he that is spiritual judgeth all things, yet he himself is judged of no man. For who hath known the mind of the Lord, that he may instruct him? But we have the mind of Christ.
                                        1 Corinthians 2:15, 16

We must *ana-krino* — use our discernment, judge what we hear and what goes on.

"Let the prophets speak two or three, and let the other *judge*."   1 Corinthians 14:29

The men of the church are to judge anyone who claims to give prophecies from God. Christian men today should publicly judge the "prophets" who started the Mormons, the Seventh Day Adventists, the Jehovah's Witnesses, Bahai etc. Christian men are commanded to *ana-krino* — judge what is said, judge what is taught. If you refuse to use

---

[1] We learned this teaching on judging from Jewish Bible teacher Jacob Prasch, of Moriel Ministries, and you can find it on the web at *www.moriel.org*.

this God-given authority now, why should the Lord give you a position of authority in His 1000 year reign? There are many standing up today claiming to be prophets, and Christian men must judge what they say. Deuteronomy 18:20–22 teaches us the test of a true prophet, that what he prophesies must come true; otherwise he is a false prophet.

Dia-krino — to decide. You should decide disputes within the Body of Christ, the assembly. You should not sue each other in civil court cases.

> **"I speak to your shame. Is it so, that there is not a wise man among you? No, not one that shall be able to judge between his brethren?"**   1 Cor 6:5

This means not to sue in *civil* court. It does NOT mean to cover up crimes that should be heard in criminal court. Great wisdom and discernment is needed here. Some churches have covered up crimes which should have been reported to the police. Paedophilia in the Roman Catholic Church is the glaring example. Hiding the crimes and protecting the priests and the reputation of the Roman church was put above the clear duty of protecting children from molestation. These on-going crimes clearly needed to be reported and dealt with.

Kritikos — to critically examine, analyze, think for yourself, weigh things up. We must examine and critically analyze what is said and taught and done in our churches. Of course, this does not mean to criticize people for every little thing, but when it is something important, we have to analyze.

Hypo-krites — hypocritical judging; judging other people for something we are also guilty of. This we are forbidden to do. Before you open your mouth to judge someone else, stop and ask yourself if you are doing the same thing yourself. If you judge someone hypocritically, for a sin that you are also committing, you **will** be judged, publicly exposed as a hypocrite. This is the word the Lord Jesus used in Matthew 7:1 when He said: "Judge not (hypocritically), that ye be not judged." Be very careful what you judge people for!

Krisis, krina — eternal judgement, heaven or hell, on the basis of belief in the Lord Jesus or rejection of Him. This judgement is not for us, but for Christ alone. Not even the Father judges anyone, for He has given all judgement to the Son. John 5:22

There are two judgement seats in the Bible: The Greek words are *thronos* and *bema*.

- **Thronos**. For the unsaved. Unsaved people will be judged at the Great White Throne of Revelation 20:11–14, where the degrees of punishment are determined, and, since all these people (most of whom thought of themselves as being good) have rejected the Lord Jesus, they are cast into the lake of fire.

- **Bema Seat**. (pronounced bee-ma) For Christians. This is the judgement seat of Christ, 1 Cor 3:12–15, where rewards for service will be given. The *bema* was where rulers in ancient Greece handed out rewards to Olympic winners; this is a type of the mercy seat in the Holy of Holies, where mercy covered the Ark of the Covenant, with the Law — the 10 Commandments — inside it. The Lord's great mercy covers all the sins of all those who put their trust in Him. We should be serving the Lord now in whatever way He gives us, so that we lay up some treasure in heaven and so that we can get some reward at His judgement seat. The private things which no one but God sees will no doubt get great rewards. These rewards are not for our achievements, but for our faithfulness in whatever the Lord has given us to do, whether it be raising children, cleaning the church, preaching etc.

Here are some relevant scriptures.

"Judge not according to the appearance, but judge righteous judgment."   John 7:24

"For I verily, as absent in body, but present in spirit, have judged already, as though I were present, concerning him that hath so done this deed."   1 Cor 5:3

"I speak as to wise men; judge ye what I say."
                                                      1 Cor 10:15

"Let two or three prophets speak and let the others pass judgement (diakrino)."   1 Cor 14:29

Other relevant words:

Gnome (pronounced no-may) — to give an opinion.

"Now concerning virgins I have no commandment of the Lord: yet I give my judgment ..."   1 Cor 7:25

Paul was careful to draw a distinction between his own opinion and doctrinal commands of God.

Di-kaioma (pronounced die-kay-oh-ma) — to give a judgement opinion, pontificate, to give a judicial opinion. Christians should certainly be judging by giving their judicial opinions on many matters in the world today.

Wolves on the prowl — a warning to the sisters!

Ladies beware. Sorry to have to put this in the book, but there is a type of man on the prowl in evangelical circles who is looking for women with money or property. This is a word of warning, because this is happening, and if you are on your own, you are vulnerable and you should be forearmed. Do not be taken in by someone who comes into your life and seems very spiritual, and very caring, but can leave you sadder, wiser, and a lot poorer.

Some signs to watch for:

- You've only just met a man, maybe at a church function, and suddenly it's your responsibility to fund him.
- He's so spiritual that he doesn't work.
- He has "heard from God" that you are to give him quite a lot of money or sign something over to him. Don't.
- He may be temporarily homeless and just needs to move in for a while (like the rest of his life).
- If you will only provide the cash, he can buy a place to ride out the End Times.
- He just needs the deposit on a property where people will all be safe.
- Then he needs the rest of the money to complete the purchase.
- If you don't come up with the cash, he quotes scripture (out of context) all day long trying to make you feel guilty.
- He wants you to keep all your conversations confidential and not tell anyone else, and he has excuses for this secrecy (the real reason is that an outsider will see right through him!).

Needless to say, you should have nothing to do with such a person, no matter how spiritual he claims to be! If you are a single woman and this type of pseudo spiritual man tries to latch on to you:

- Don't see him on your own; always have a Christian friend with you, someone with their brain switched on.
- If he asks you for a large sum of money, get your pastor or a leader at church involved, because wisdom comes with many counsellors. You need some back-up.

- A man on his own should go and live somewhere else, not with you.
- It is not your responsibility to fund him or house him. At best, he is misguided, but most probably he is just a leech and a scoundrel.

There's another type of wolf around, under the cloak of a "financial advisor". They are not all like this, but some are. Your husband has died, leaving you money and property, and now you have "financial advisors" calling you or writing or otherwise trying to get themselves into your life and your bank balance. Be aware that they will charge a large percentage for anything they do. They will manage your money all right — manage to make it disappear in some cases.

So what do you do? Trust your own accountant and mature Christian brothers to advise you and to check out anybody who wants to manage your money.

Chapter 19

You MUST Be Born Again

The Lord Jesus spoke these words to Nicodemus, a leader of the Jews: "Except a man be born again, he cannot see the kingdom of God." *Gospel of John Chapter 3 verse 3* Nicodemus puzzled as to how this could be; how could he, a grown man, be born all over again?

The Lord Jesus said: "Except a man be born of water AND the Spirit, he cannot enter the kingdom of God. "That which is born of the flesh is flesh, and that which is born of the Spirit is spirit." When you are born as a baby, you are born of water. Babies in the womb are surrounded and cushioned by water. When the "waters break", it is time for the baby to be born, and every woman knows, as soon as her waters break — this is it! The baby's on the way! We are ALL born of water. But Jesus said we also have to be born of the Holy Spirit.

So the Lord Jesus was saying that in order to get into His kingdom, people HAVE to be born all over again, not born physically as a baby again, but born spiritually. This new *spiritual* birth is something God Himself does, giving us His Holy Spirit when we believe in Jesus, and causing our spirit within us to come alive. Ephesians 1:13 tells us that when we believe, we are "sealed with the Holy Spirit..."

Until we are born again spiritually, the Bible tells us that our spirits are dead — we are spiritually dead. We are physically alive, but our spirits are dead.

The Lord reminded Nicodemus of Moses, who led the Israelites out of Egypt. The Israelites were miraculously fed each day with manna from Heaven. They got sick of eating manna every day and grumbled about it. God was so fed up with them that He allowed snakes to invade their camp and many died from snakebites. When Moses prayed urgently to the Lord for a solution, he was told to make a brass image of a snake and put it up on a pole. All the people who were bitten by snakes would be saved if they just looked at the snake on the pole.

The Lord Jesus said a similar thing was going to happen in Israel. He Himself would be "lifted up" and everyone who looked to Him for their salvation, everyone who believed in Him, would not perish, but have eternal life. They would be saved. They would be born again spiritually.

He told Nicodemus the most famous words in the Bible:

"For God so loved the world that He gave His only begotten Son, that whosoever believes in Him should not perish, but have everlasting life." John 3:16

Like the Israelites in the desert, people now are in danger of dying and missing out on Heaven. The Bible says none of us is good enough *(Romans 3:10)*. We are all born with an inclination to sin, and we all do sin, to a greater or lesser extent. Some people commit very big sins. Some people commit lesser sins, but all sin is disgusting in God's sight.

The Lord Jesus said the one and only way to Heaven was through Him. He said:

"I am the way, the truth, and the life. No one comes to the Father except through Me." John 14:6

That is why we have to put our faith and trust in Jesus. Then we can be born again of the Holy Spirit.

Here is a good prayer:

Lord Jesus, I believe in You. I believe that You are the Son of God and You died on the cross to pay the price for all our sins. I know that You were buried and rose from the dead after three days. I put my trust in You. Please forgive my sins. Please make me one of Your people.

It is up to you

We have tried to set out the main false religions in the world today, contrasting them with the truth. Academics tend to leave the false religions alone, while fiercely attacking Christianity and the Bible at every turn. If you are a Christian reading this, we hope it equips you better to contend for the faith, as Jude, the half brother of the Lord, exhorted us in his epistle. If you are in a false religion, we pray that your eyes will be opened and you will have the courage to leave it — and it does take courage. There might be a cost involved, but, if that is the case with you, take heart. God is no man's debtor. Any cost to you now will seem very small when the Lord hands out rewards to His people.

Afterword

Alan Franklin writes:

Pat and I hope you have found this book informative. It is designed as a cutting tool to carve through the phoney claims of false faiths.

Here I would like to pay tribute to some great men of God who have inspired and helped us and without whom we would know a lot less and be less able to discern truth from error.

First must come (Doctors) Noah Hutchings, Bob Glaze and Larry Spargimino, of South West Radio Church of Oklahoma, *(www.swrc. com)* a fine, courageous Christian ministry that is steadfast in supporting Israel, expounding the prophetic word and broadcasting the truth daily on hundreds of radio stations whatever the cost. Had they not encouraged me to write my first book, *EU: Final World Empire*, we would not have gone on to write its two successors. The EU book will be rewritten, updated and reprinted in its third edition next year. Like our other teaching aids, DVDs etc, it will be available from our website, *thefreepressonline.co.uk.*

I would also like to thank Dr David Reagan of Lamb and Lion Ministries of McKinney, Texas *(www.lamblion.com)* who persuaded me to get on with writing books at a time when I was a busy newspaper editor with little taste for writing in my spare time! Dave is a great teacher and his program *Christ in Prophecy* is one of the best things on Christian TV. You can find it on Daystar and other networks.

I have used Dave's exposés of Adventism and Freemasonry as the basis for some of our research into these false beliefs and recommend all his books and DVDs.

We as a family also owe a lot to Dr. Arnold Fruchtenbaum, whose teaching camps in New York State our daughter Annie was privileged to attend for three summers, and who later flew to England to perform Annie and Michael's wedding ceremony. Arnold's book *Footsteps of The Messiah* is a common source of reference for us and is often used to settle theological disputes. We recommend that you visit Arnold's website, *www.ariel.org* and avail yourselves of his authoritative teaching materials.

Everything by Dave Hunt should be on your bookshelves and we trust The Berean Call so much that they provide live news feed to our

Christian news section and it appears without us editing it. Log on to them at *www.thebereancall.org.*

Thanks also to Jacob Prasch, for keeping us up to speed on many aspects of hermeneutics. His website, like others mentioned, is linked to ours, so just go on to *www.thefreepressonline.co.uk* and click on links. To go direct to Jacob's site, key in *www.moriel.org.*

We would also like to point people toward Doug Harris and Reachout Trust, a ministry specializing in the cults. Their website is *www. reachouttrust.org.*

Lastly, we recommend the website of our son-in-law Michael Nissim and our daughter Annie in Israel. On *www.israelunique.com* you will find some interesting articles, plus a selection of good books, music and gift items including Scripture notecards and beautiful silk scarves from Galilee.

Meanwhile, time is short and we feel great urgency in getting these truths out to a lost and dying world. If anyone is interested in obtaining bulk supplies of our books or in having me speak at their church, in America, Canada, or Great Britain, please contact me at *alan@thefree-pressonline.co.uk.*

Choose this day who you will serve.